Chicago Stained Glass

Erne R. and Florence Frueh

Photography by
Erne R. Frueh and George A. Lane, S.J.

Second Edition

Wild Onion Books

an imprint of Loyola Press
Chicago

Wild Onion Books
an imprint of Loyola Press
3441 North Ashland Avenue
Chicago, Illinois 60657

Wild Onion Books publishes provocative titles on Chicago themes that offer diverse perspectives on the city and surrounding area, its history, its culture, and its religions. Wild onion is a common nickname for Chicago.

Publication of this book was supported by a grant from the Graham Foundation for Advanced Studies in the Fine Arts.

The illustrations from the book *The Second Presbyterian Church of Chicago, Art and Architecture* by Erne R. and Florence Frueh are reprinted with permission.

The illustrations *Head of Christ* and *Cloister Window, Aachen Cathedral* taken from *Stained Glass* by Lawrence Lee, George Seddon, and Francis Stephens. Copyright by permission of Crown Publishers, Inc.

Cover design by Amy Olson
Cover photo by George A. Lane, S.J.

Library of Congress Cataloging-in-Publication Data

Frueh, Erne R., 1912-
    Chicago stained glass / Erne R. and Florence Frueh ; photography by Erne R. Frueh and George A. Lane.—2nd ed.
        p.   cm.
    Includes bibliographical references and index.
    ISBN   0-8294-1030-9
    1. Glass painting and staining—Illinois—Chicago—History.   2. Glass painting and staining—History.
I. Frueh, Florence, 1912-   . II. Title.
NK5312.F75   1998
748.59173'11—dc21   97-31944
                                          CIP

To our daughters Renee and Joanna

Angel with lute. SS. Cyril and Methodius Church, 50th and
South Hermitage Avenue. The Munich Studio, Chicago, 1913.
Width, 8 feet. The church is now closed.

Contents

Preface

Until about ten years ago our greatest interest in colored glass revolved about the beautiful vases, bowls, and drinking vessels produced during the "Golden Age of Art Glass" in the late nineteenth and early twentieth centuries. We studied the work of the Austrian firm Loetz-Witwe, the Englishman John Northwood, the Frenchman Emile Gallé, the American Louis Comfort Tiffany, and the equally intriguing work of lesser known glass artists and designers. A number of our articles about these men and their work appeared in collectors and antiques magazines.

Then abruptly—and quite accidentally—our interest switched to stained glass windows and we have been researching, photographing, and writing about these hidden but public treasures in Chicago ever since.

The sudden change occurred while we were seeking information on the influence of William Morris and the English Arts and Crafts Movement on Chicago artists and designers at the turn of the century. In our search we stumbled upon Edward Wagenknecht's book, *Chicago,* in which the author mentions two windows at the Second Presbyterian Church which were designed by Sir Edward Burne-Jones and executed by the firm of William Morris.

We knew of Burne-Jones, the eminent Pre-Raphaelite painter who was the close friend of William Morris, the leading figure in the English Arts and Crafts Movement. And we knew that the two men formed what has been called an "inspired partnership" to produce stained glass windows.

Christ Blessing the Little Children. *Second Presbyterian Church, 1936 South Michigan Avenue. Tiffany Studios, 1893. Width, 9 feet.*

Excited by the possibility that there might indeed be examples of the Englishmen's work "living and breathing" in Chicago, we visited the Second Presbyterian Church on South Michigan Avenue. The Rev. Joe E. Francis answered our eager questions about the windows with disconcerting casualness: "Oh, yes, the windows you want to see are in the vestibule." But entering the sanctuary through a doorway near the pulpit, it was necessary to walk through the nave to reach the vestibule. On that first of many subsequent walks, Joe frequently reminds us, we exclaimed: "Wow! Tiffany windows."

In addition to fourteen windows by Tiffany there was also one attributed to John La Farge of New York City, Tiffany's chief competitor; one by Chicago's internationally known partnership of Healy & Millet; four by the city's well-respected firm of McCully & Miles; and a number designed by the prominent Chicago architect Howard Van Doren Shaw. And in the vestibule, radiant in the morning light, were the English gems, studies of St. Margaret and St. Cecilia.

We silently thanked Wagenknecht for his invaluable lead and decided that Chicagoans ought to know of this gallery of stained glass art. We made numerous visits to the church to photograph the windows in just the proper light. Joe Francis put the church archives at our disposal and with outside research on the glassmen, their styles, the glasses they used, as well as on the windows' wealthy donors, we wrote and illustrated an article for *Chicago History* magazine. Fannia Weingartner, the publication's editor at the time, encouraged us to continue to uncover other examples of the city's little known stained glass treasures.

While photographing more local stained glass, we met Father Charles Kouba, pastor of SS. Cyril and Methodius Church, who asked us to photograph the stained glass of his church for a forthcoming anniversary celebration.

The windows at Father Kouba's church were far different from most we had seen, including those at Second Presbyterian. In the latter, for example, Tiffany's and La Farge's works were composed of thick, semi-opaque American opalescent glass, little painted. Healy & Millet's and McCully & Miles' were fabricated of internally and externally textured cathedral glass, also little painted. Shaw's, entirely absent of paint, were defined only by leadlines and were constructed of either lightly tinted green antique glass or various colors of slightly textured cathedral glass. The Burne-Jones and William Morris windows were made of luminous English antique glass lightly painted. But the SS. Cyril and Methodius windows were composed of French and German antique glass heavily painted with dark oxides, but so skillfully that none of the glass lambency was lost. Moreover, they were in the German Baroque style and certainly the work of a single artist.

The various glasses, styles, and techniques we had seen so intrigued us that by the time we finished photographing the windows at Father Kouba's church our interest in vases and bowls went into limbo. Stained glass had hooked us.

We used ladders to photograph certain details of the SS. Cyril and Methodius windows and discovered that each was signed "Munich Studio, Chicago." This was an exceptional find, for most Chicago glassmen and outsiders as well, even including Tiffany and La Farge, rarely signed or dated their windows.

Subsequently, during a visit with Frank J. Drehobl, Jr., dean of Chicago's glassmen and president of the Drehobl Bros. Art Glass Co., we learned that Max Guler, a German immigrant artist, was the founder of the Munich Studio. From Drehobl's collection of old Munich Studio catalogs, we further learned that Guler had windows in at least thirty-five Chicago churches as well as installations nationwide. Armed with this material and additional research, we wrote and illustrated an article on the Munich Studio for *Stained Glass* magazine.

Joe Francis asked us to write and illustrate a small book on the art and architecture of the Second Presbyterian Church, which we did. Dr. Norman Temme, editor of *Stained Glass,* always interested in our findings and pictures, published several of our articles. Lectures to local organizations led to our participation in the symposium at the 1982 exhibition of Tiffany art at the Museum of Science and Industry in Chicago in which we spoke about "Tiffany and Chicago Stained Glass."

Mystical Marriage of St. Catherine of Alexandria. *Our Lady of Sorrows Basilica, 3121 West Jackson Boulevard; formerly in Presentation Church. Munich Studio, Chicago, 1909. Width. approx. 60 inches.*

Considerably before that event, however, Sharon S. Darling, curator of Decorative Art at the Chicago Historical Society, requested our participation in a bus tour of some city churches to discuss their window art. It was on that delightful occasion that we met Father George A. Lane who was then in the midst of writing his book *Chicago Churches and Synagogues.* Subsequently, Father Lane asked us to write an essay on ecclesiastical glass for his forthcoming publication. We accepted his invitation.

After the publication of his work, George, as associate director of Loyola University Press, urged us to write a book expanding upon our essay. We would, we said, if we could develop a history of stained glass in Chicago which would include secular as well as ecclesiastical stained glass art. George was delighted with the idea.

After clearing our desks of a partially written but uncommitted article on that unique Chicago stained glass artist, Thomas Augustin O'Shaughnessy, we went to work on this book.

Acknowledgments

We are deeply grateful to the many pastors, rabbis, and their staffs who so graciously arranged for us to photograph the windows of their houses of worship. Administrators of public buildings were equally cooperative, though several were bemused that we actually wanted to photograph "those old windows."

We especially wish to thank Sharon Darling, author of *Chicago Ceramics and Glass,* who not only gave generously of her knowledge but also granted us access to the Chicago Historical Society's files on stained glass by local artists and studios. Others on the staff of the Chicago Historical Society who patiently assisted us in our research were Grant T. Dean, assistant curator of Private Collections, and Julia Westerberg, formerly assistant curator of the Graphics Department.

At the Art Institute of Chicago, Cecilia Chin, and before her Annette Fern, assistant librarians at the Burnham and Ryerson libraries, helped us to track down important information in art, architecture, and industrial arts magazines during the years when Chicago was a major stained glass center. Jean F. Block, president of Midway Editorial Research; Rolf Achilles, assistant director and registrar of the University of Chicago's Smart Gallery; and Alfred Tannler, former archivist of the Regenstein Library at the University of Chicago, gave us documents and information about stained glass windows in the university's campus buildings.

Chicago glassmen Frank J. Drehobl, Jr., Lubomyr Wandzura, Adolfas Valeska, Bob White, William Klopsch, and Craig Corbin cooperated enthusiastically, as did Joseph O'Shaughnessy, the son of glass artist Thomas O'Shaughnessy, who loaned us many valuable documents concerning his father's work.

Father George Lane made many sorties into the field to discover and photograph windows. Had it not been for his enthusiasm and expert photography more than one important example of the art would have been missing from this book.

We wish to thank Chicago's Graham Foundation for Advanced Studies in the Fine Arts for a generous grant to assist in the reproduction of color plates for this publication and its director, Carter H. Manny, Jr., for his interest in this project.

Assistance also came from many quarters outside of Chicago: Dr. Norman Temme, editor of *Stained Glass;* Helene Weis, librarian of the Willett Stained Glass Studios; Kai Ketcham, secretary to Connick Associates; Bernard E. Gruenke, president of the Conrad schmitt Studio; Robert Frei, president of Emil Frei Associates; Geoffrey Melcher, retired General manager of the Conrad Pickel Studio; and Robert Kehlmann and Kenneth von Roenn, distinguished stained glass artists and writers.

Notes on Photography

Each time one of our articles appeared in print or during question and answer periods following lectures, questions concerning stained glass photography arose. Actually, there is nothing magical about this type of photography that time and patience will not overcome. However, readers and listeners alike want to know about the type of camera we use, the film, the props, and time exposures.

We rely on a 35mm Nikkormat EL and George Lane uses a Pentax ME super and a Zensa Bronica camera. The three lenses we find indispensable are: a 50mm-1:1.4 for general shots; a wide angle 24mm-1:1.2 for architectonic shots; and a telescopic 135mm-1:2.8 for details or to bring distant subjects into a larger format without distortion. Our film for color is Kodachrome 64 because it is slow, and from experimentation we find that it provides better color saturation than faster films. Father Lane uses Ektachrome 200.

Other than these essentials we use in all instances a sturdy tripod, match folders to place under the tripod to correct the camera position on uneven floors, and a cable shutter release to keep the camera from moving while the shutter is being pressed. Under no circumstances do we use light modulators such as bank lights, aluminum screens, or canvas or paper sheets for backlighting. Natural light, we think, is best because it gives a truer picture of the window and the artist's intent.

Rather than a bright day, we prefer a slightly overcast one for picture-taking jaunts. This, we feel, shows the nuances of the glass to best advantage. We avoid shooting opalescent windows when light passing through them is at an angle, for such a condition often casts a halo about images or "burns" spots on the negative. Also, in general, we avoid whenever possible shooting windows from angles because the horizontal and vertical crossbars supporting them appear too prominent and create distortion.

So much depends upon the quality of the light that there is no standard for lens openings and shutter speeds. On a slightly overcast day, we open the lens to 5.6, and trusting the electronic eye for shutter speeds (which usually vary between a thirtieth and a sixtieth of a second) focus and shoot. Then we shoot a frame one stop over and one stop under the 5.6 opening. This "bracketing" of frames provides a measure of insurance in obtaining the "perfect" exposure.

Light causes the colors of stained glass to vary constantly—sometimes within a few seconds. Thus as windows are revisited from time to time they will appear different, for remembered brilliancies and subtle nuances in color will have disappeared and new ones will have replaced them. So photographers will never realize the perfect negative. But they, like the reader, will find that the changing colors make each revisit to favorite windows a renewed delight, and for the photographer a constant challenge.

Introduction

This study does not pretend to be the definitive one on stained glass in Chicago. With thousands of stained glass windows existing in most of the city's over two thousand houses of worship and in some turn-of-the-century public buildings and residences, documenting them alone would require the lifetimes of an indefatigable corps of research assistants, writers, and photographers.

Rather, our more modest aim is to introduce the reader to the rich and diverse stained glass treasures to be found throughout the city's vast public museum of the art. If this study succeeds in eliciting an interest in and appreciation for the manifold joys of stained glass and stimulates further explorations of the art in Chicago, we will have been amply rewarded.

To assist the general reader and the stained glass devotee, there is appended to the text a list of documented works, by no means complete, and the buildings in which they are located. Explorations beyond the list will frequently uncover other treasures, for there are hundreds only waiting to be discovered. In only a few instances have windows of suburban buildings been included, and these only to round out the work of a particular artist or studio.

Dome in the lobby of the G.A.R. rooms. Chicago Public Library Cultural Center, 78 East Washington Street. Tiffany Studios, 1897. Diameter, 40 feet.

Research for much of the second chapter of this book was difficult, for there are no books previous to this one completely devoted to stained glass in Chicago. Sharon S. Darling's excellent and pioneering *Chicago Ceramics and Glass* by its nature is limited only to Chicago glassmen and takes the reader only to 1933. David A. Hanks' *The Decorative Designs of Frank Lloyd Wright* is limited to the stained glass studios which executed the architect's work. Our own contributions to *Stained Glass* and *Chicago History* magazines are confined to the work of a single artist or studio or the windows in a particular building.

Because of the disappearance of most of Chicago's earlier glass firms and their records and the neglect of stained glass over the years, our sources of information were most varied. They range from city directories, guide books published for the socially elite, architectural periodicals, personal papers, interviews, and numerous books on topics seemingly unrelated to stained glass but containing fascinating references to the decoration during the years when Chicago was an important center for glass art.

From these diverse sources, which often led to dead ends, we were able to gather only snatches of information with which to piece together the story of the city's stained glass and those of its fabricators. Rarely was it possible to develop extended continuities of these stories.

Another problem for the stained glass historian is that of window identification, for few earlier glassmen felt the need to sign or date their work. This makes attributions difficult or virtually impossible, particularly in windows where the styles or the glasses used were similar. Research on firms outside of Chicago was much easier because many of these establishments are still in business and have kept adequate records.

The tremendous revival of interest in stained glass since the 1960s has made the stained glass historian's task easier. Many more studios now sign and date their work and keep records of their activities while houses of worship include in their booklets and brochures information and descriptions of their stained glass art.

Indeed, because of the revival, Chicagoans in general have perceived the importance of this hitherto neglected segment of the city's public art and are preserving and protecting it as one of their richest cultural legacies.

Historical Background 1

Detail, Notre Dame de la Belle Verriere. *Chartres Cathedral, France. 12th century.*

Chapter One

Because it is bound to architecture and because of the unpredictable behavior of light, stained glass has always presented special problems for the artist working in that medium. Unlike the painter who can predetermine the size of his canvas and choose his colors at will, the stained glass artist must work within the architectural framework, always aware that his choice of colors, even in the best of circumstances, will change constantly depending on the quality of the light, the time of day, and the season of the year.

Yet despite these restrictions, or because of them, artists have created the great stained glass masterpieces of the twelfth and thirteen centuries and, equaling them in emotional force and splendor, the magnificent works of the twentieth century. Far from being a "lost art," stained glass is today more alive than ever before in its long and eventful history.

Ancient Origins

Windows of transparent glass were first used in the houses and villas of wealthy Romans and in the palaces of the emperors in the first century A.D. As the remains of windows excavated at Pompeii and Herculaneum attest, Roman windows consisted of a lattice of small panes of clear or colored glass held together with narrow strips of wood, copper, or lead.

As an artistic medium, however, rather than a domestic luxury of Roman times, the evolution of stained glass was a slow and uneven process that developed gradually following Constantine's edict of 313 A.D. which permitted Christians to build churches and worship openly.

Having no churches of their own, the Christians for their architecture adopted elements from the Roman rectangular basilica and the Byzantine central domical plan. An example of the latter was the great church of Santa Sophia in Constantinople (537 A.D.) which had windows of perforated alabaster set with jewel-like colored glass "exceeding in splendor anything that had before been seen."

Romanesque Churches

By the ninth and tenth centuries, to accommodate the needs of the ever-growing congregations and clergy, the simple cruciform plan of the earliest Christian churches had been enlarged to include double transepts, choirs, ambulatories, side aisles, balconies, and private chapels. Known as the Romanesque style, its principal features were massive walls and piers, intersecting vaults, elaborately carved tympana, and round-arched windows and doors.

Detail of picture on page 17.

Usually, so as not to weaken the thick walls supporting the enormous weight of the barrel-vaulted stone roofs, the windows were small and few and closed with brick, wood, or cement. To admit light, however, some were filled with thin sheets of alabaster, marble, or even wooden boards which were pierced, and the holes inserted with small pieces of colored glass arranged in simple geometric patterns of diamonds, circles, or squares. Rather than stained glass, the principal interior decorations of these churches were the splendid mosaics and murals depicting saints, biblical personages, and events from the Old and New Testaments.

Although the production of glass had been a flourishing industry in Roman times, the disintegration of the Roman Empire during the fourth and fifth centuries caused many glassworkers to gravitate to the region of the Rhine and Rhone valleys where the materials for making glass—sand, firewood, and ash—as well as trade routes for transporting the finished product were readily available. By the close of the seventh century, if not before, France had established a substantial glass industry, even exporting glass to England where French artisans instructed the English in the stained glass craft.

In the sixth century, some of the more progressive clergy had already begun to install entire windows of clear or colored glass in their churches and abbeys; most notably in France Gregory of Tours for St. Martin of Tours and in England in the following century (c. 675) Abbot Benedict Biscop of Monkwearmouth, who sent for French glaziers to execute the windows of his monastery church. How these windows were designed or constructed we have no way of knowing, for the St. Martin windows have not survived, and the pieces of red, blue, green, and amber glass excavated at Monkwearmouth show no trace of painted design.

Gaps in the early history of stained glass make it virtually impossible to pinpoint when the first figural-narrative windows appeared. But it is definitely known that toward the close of the tenth century, when the cathedral at Reims was rebuilt, Bishop Adalberon graced it with windows picturing biblical scenes. These windows were milestones in the development of stained glass, for they not only served a didactic function, but were the first we know of in which painted glass was used to delineate the human form, to control the light, and to modulate color effects.

Actually, the term stained glass is misleading, for rather than being "stained," the glass is colored throughout by metallic oxides already in the glass or by chemicals infused into the glass while it is still molten. It may also be painted with vitreous enamels composed of dark brown or black metallic oxides and ground glass which are fired onto the glass surface.

Leaded pictorial glass is thought to have been suggested by the earlier arts of mosaics, goldsmithing, and enameling. Especially suited for transference to stained glass was the art of enameling known as cloisonné. In this art thin strips of metal are soldered sidewise to a groundwork and the spaces between them filled with colored enamel made of powdered glass. The enamel is then fused to the groundwork in a furnace at low heat, thus separating each color from the metal strips, a process very like that used in the making of stained glass.

The earliest extant examples of painted pictorial glass are heads of Christ: one of the ninth or tenth century excavated from Lorsch Abbey in Germany, the other from the abbey church in Wissembourg, Alsace, now in the museum at Strasbourg. The most famous examples, dating from the eleventh century, are in the clerestory of the cathedral at Augsburg, Germany. These are the series of five panels of the prophets Moses, Daniel, David, Jonas, and Hosea — austere, rigidly posed frontal figures attired in stiff robes of brown, wine, gold, green, and pale blue, the colors characteristic of stained glass windows in German churches of the Romanesque period.

Gothic Cathedrals

Although the windows at Augsburg display amazing artistry and technical skill, stained glass was still a budding art form until the mid-twelfth century, when it suddenly burst into full bloom with the advent of Gothic architecture. With its slim piers supporting lacy flying buttresses, delicate ribbed vaulting and pointed arches, the revolutionary Gothic style soared to lofty heights, opening up immense expanses of window space filled, like those at Chartres and Sainte Chapelle, with glowing stained glass pictures relating the stories of the Scriptures to the faithful, most of whom could neither read nor write.

The passionate religious zeal which built the great Gothic cathedrals was inspired by a love of God and His universe and an extraordinary devotion to the Virgin Mary unparalleled in history. It was an age of exuberance, of a rebirth of the human spirit after the "long dark" of the barbarian invasions, when decimated towns were rebuilt, social life resumed, and trade guilds and universities founded.

In their eagerness to serve God, princes, peasants, and beggars alike yoked themselves to carts to haul loads of stones and provisions long distances to the construction sites of churches and cathedrals. Haymo, the abbot of St. Pierre-sur-Dives, who must have witnessed many such scenes, recounts: "We may see this miracle, that although sometimes a thousand men and women, or even more, are bound to the traces (so vast is the mass, so great is the engine, and so heavy the load laid upon it), yet they go forward in such silence that no voice, no murmur is heard . . ."[1]

Above:

Head of Christ. *10th century.
From Wissemburg Abbey, Alsace;
now in the Musee de l' Oeuvre
Notre Dame, Strasbourg. Note:
Photographed from* Stained Glass
*by Lawrence Lee, et. al. Crown
Publishers, 1976.*

Right:

David, *from the five prophet
windows. Augsburg Cathedral,
Germany. 11th century.*

Of the ecclesiastics of his time, none was more innovative than the renowned Abbot Suger, who rose from lowly birth to be the counselor to kings and who in 1140-44 rebuilt the abbey church of St. Denis, the prototype of Gothic architecture. Inspired by the metaphysical writings of the Neo-Platonists and the Syrian mystic Dionysius the Areopagite, Suger conceived of light as a spiritual force which transmitted through the radiance of stained glass, would "illumine men's minds . . . to an apprehension of God's light," and so to direct communion with Him.

Thus, in replacing the abbey's windows to his purpose, Suger, as he wrote, "caused to be painted by the exquisite hands of many masters from different regions a splendid variety of new windows," for which he personally selected the themes and colors. Suger loved the luminous "sapphire blue" glass of St. Denis, and it is thought that he was instrumental in choosing the same color and glass for the earliest windows at Chartres and also their designs and subjects. Most of the St. Denis windows were destroyed in 1793 during the French Revolution. Some, however, were rescued and in 1848 restored, cognoscenti say too heavily, by Viollet-le-Duc, the French architect-historian. Fragments and entire windows still exist in collections and churches throughout Europe.

Curtain walls of glass, composed of medallions. Sainte Chapelle, Paris, France. 13th century.

Suger's ardor for his new stained glass windows knew no bounds and in contemplation of their beauty he ecstatically wrote: "When the house of God, many colored as the radiance of precious stones, called me from the cares of the world . . . I seemed to find myself, as it were, in some strange part of the universe, which was neither wholly of the baseness of the earth, nor wholly of the serenity of heaven; but by the grace of God, I seemed lifted in some mystic manner from this lower, toward that upper sphere."[2] If the abbot could be so transported, the effect on the people must have been overwhelming.

How was it possible for medieval glassmen to evoke such exaltation with their limited choice of materials and colors? Needless to say there were among them gifted artists and master craftsmen who had learned through trial and error to use their resources to the maximum. Above all was their uncanny sense of how to use color for the most subtle and rich tonal relationships. For example, instead of simply choosing a piece of purple glass, small chips of red and blue glass might be placed side by side so that from a distance, as in an impressionist painting, they mixed in the beholder's eye to create a more vibrant color effect.

Their first concern was color, and as Henry Adams wrote: "They never hesitated to put their colour where they wanted it, or cared whether a green camel or a pink lion looked like a dog or donkey provided they got their harmony or value . . . So we laugh to see a knight with a blue face, on a green horse, that looks as though drawn by a four-year-old child, and probably the artist laughed too; but he was a colourist, and never sacrificed his colour for a laugh."[3]

Medieval Glass

Exactly how twelfth and thirteenth century craftsmen made glass and fabricated windows has been fully recorded in *De Diversis Artium,* an exhaustive treatise on various of the decorative arts written by the German monk Theophilus in the early twelfth century. In the more than eight hundred years since Theophilus made his observations, the procedures for making a stained glass window scarcely differ from those in use today. The only differences come from such mechanical improvements as steel-wheel glass cutters in place of the old dividing iron, plate glass easels in lieu of the whitewashed board, and gas and electric soldering irons.

Medieval stained glass artists and craftsmen worked closely with the architect, often setting up their workshops at the site of the church under construction. There, in large crucibles, they mixed their ingredients—basically sand, potash, and lime for white or clear glass and oxides for color. Copper, for example, produced ruby; oxide of iron, green or yellow; cobalt, blue; and manganese, purple. The entire mixture was then fired far beyond the melting point to produce the colored pot metal glass similar to the commercial or handblown "antique glass" made today.

When the desired color was obtained, the glassblower had a choice of making either "crown" or "muff" glass. For crown glass he gathered a glob of molten glass on a blowpipe and blew it into a cylinder which he slit lengthwise down one side and twirled before the heat of the furnace until it expanded into a disc thicker at the center than at the perimeter. He then tapped the disc off the blowpipe. For muff glass he followed the same procedure, but after slitting the cylinder and tapping it off the pipe, he flattened it with an iron rod. It seems that with either method the outside dimensions of the disc or flattened sheet of glass was about ten or twelve inches.

Next the glass was placed on an iron sheet and put into a furnace at low heat to anneal. After it had cooled slowly and hardened, the glass was cut into small pieces to fit over each numbered part of a cartoon (a prepared drawing of a window design) which had been sketched on a whitewashed board. Facial features, hair, hands, feet, drapery folds, and other details too small to render with chips of glass were painted on the glass with viscous black or yellow brown oxides, which for subtler tones and shading were diluted with wine or water.

Each piece was then numbered with its corresponding number on the cartoon, removed from the board, and placed in the furnace for refiring. This permanently bonded the painted portions to the glass. When cooled, the pieces were reassembled according to their numbers on the board, fastened with H-shaped strips of lead called cames, and soldered at each joint. Spaces between the glass and the lead were filled with putty or cement, which strengthened and weatherproofed the window and also emphasized the design. Finally, after being thoroughly cleaned, the window was carried to the aperture, cemented into the wood or stone frame, and additionally secured by horizontal iron bars.

Medieval glass was imperfect at best, varying in thickness as well as texture. Often the glass was rough and uneven and craftsmen had no way to prevent air bubbles, impurity specks, and small annealing cracks. But these defects, if they can be called that, gave additional brilliance and dimension to the glass. In fact, glassmen deliberately seek such imperfections for the same effects today.

Only a few developments in stained glass color techniques have evolved since the time of Theophilus and Abbot Suger. In the thirteenth century grisaille work (a method of painting foliate or geometric designs on clear or white glass) was introduced to subdue light and also, in some instances, to reduce costs when colored glass became too expensive.

In the fourteenth century it was found that silver nitrate or "yellow stain" painted onto the glass in different densities and fired at different temperatures produced colors ranging from pale yellow to rich dark yellow, or even burnt sienna. This revolutionary discovery made it possible to paint, for example, a head, hair, and a halo on the same piece of glass, thus reducing the number of leadlines in a window.

An important innovation made in the fifteenth century was flashed glass. This was glass with a thin film of color on one or both sides, usually ruby or blue, which when rubbed with powdered stone exposed the clear or white glass beneath. Since the nineteenth century this laborious and time-consuming method has been much facilitated by using hydrofluoric acid to eat or etch away unwanted portions of the glass. "Except for this late refinement," as Robert Sowers has pointed out, "all of the practicable methods of color manipulation now known were perfected in the Middle Ages."[4]

Decline and Destruction

The beauty and power of medieval stained glass lasted for about three hundred years. But beginning in the 1500s the survival of the art was seriously jeopardized by political and religious upheavals, wars, and, ironically enough, its own practitioners.

Although much stained glass was destroyed in Europe during the Reformation in attacks on the Roman Catholic Church, the damage was most severe in England. In 1534 after Henry VIII's break with Rome, laws were enacted for the destruction of all monasteries, the ostensible reason being that they were centers of "manifest sin, vicious, carnal, and abominable living." Many windows were melted down for their lead, which was then used for shot and armaments.

In 1547 all churches were compelled to "utterly extinct" stained glass windows and "all other monuments of feigned miracles, pilgrimages, idolatry and superstition; so that there remain no memory of same in walls, glass windows or elsewhere."[5] The violence and destruction continued during the reigns of Edward VI and Queen Elizabeth, despite the latter's attempt to bar the Protestant Reformers from breaking or defacing church windows, "offenders being liable to be committed to prison . . ."

Under the Commonwealth in England (1642-1653), stained glass windows by the thousands were shattered in "righteous indignation" by the Puritans who deemed them manifestations of "self-indulgence" and "the fruits and occasions of idolatry."

In 1633 the province of Lorraine in France, where most of the factories for making colored glass were located, was devastated by war and the factories and furnaces razed to the ground. Since the production of colored glass virtually ceased, glassworkers began to paint on clear glass with colored enamels. Avoiding religious imagery because of the severe penalties that were imposed, they resorted to making small heraldic panels for secular use. These became extremely popular and were produced in great numbers, particularly in Switzerland, the Netherlands, and Germany.

Moreover, as Renaissance architecture took precedence over the Gothic style throughout much of Europe, the use of stained glass further declined. Based on classical Greek and Roman forms, the new style's extensive stretches of wall space, as in Romanesque architecture, were conducive to mural painting, relegating stained glass to a secondary role.

But the severest setback to the art came from seventeenth and eighteenth century artists and glaziers who, emulating such masters of mural and easel painting as Botticelli, Giotto, Michelangelo, Raphael, and Piero della Francesca, brushed thick, dulling enamels on the surface of the glass as if it were the canvas of an oil painting. Thus they destroyed the very soul of the art—its translucency.

The nadir was reached in the eighteenth century when the eminent portrait painter Sir Joshua Reynolds, as well as lesser luminaries, having little or no understanding of stained glass techniques, merely painted vapid pictures on white glass with impermanent enamels, disregarding even the leadlines so essential to the medium. Lacking the beauty and integrity of the medieval work, stained glass became a neglected and almost forgotten art.

Nineteenth Century Revival

It was the revival of Gothicism in the nineteenth century which rescued stained glass from what otherwise might have been oblivion. Playing key roles in its revitalization were Augustin Welby Pugin, Charles Winston, and William Morris in England, and Eugene Viollet-le-Duc in France.

Pugin, an architect and fanatic Gothicist, restored hundreds of medieval churches and designed hundreds of new ones in the Neo-Gothic style, including stained glass windows for a number of them. Winston, an attorney and antiquarian with a passion for stained glass, in association with James Powell and Sons, London glassmakers, produced stained glass equal to and sometimes superior to the medieval product. Winston wrote several books on medieval glass and painting styles which are still the most exhaustive on these subjects. He also translated Theophilus's treatise from the medieval Latin.

In France, Viollet-le-Duc, an Inspector-General for the newly formed *Services des Monuments Historiques,* restored hundreds of medieval buildings and their stained glass windows. While doing so, he made the first systematic analysis of color radiation in twelfth and thirteenth century stained glass, and wrote his famous essay *"Vitrail"* (1868). Viollet-le-Duc's basic conclusion, like Winston's, was that "effective stained glass depends on pure color." "This," he stressed, "had been perfectly understood and employed by the glass painters of the twelfth and thirteenth centuries, neglected from the fifteenth century on, and afterward disdained in spite of the immutable laws imposed by light and optics."

But it is to William Morris, the leader of the English Arts and Crafts Movement, that most of the credit must be given for the stained glass revival. Disheartened by the inferior workmanship and mediocre design of machine-made decorative wares, Morris, following his own precept for a return to sound medieval craftsmanship, set up workshops for the production of handmade crafts, including a studio for stained glass. Using the best materials, he trained his own craftsmen and hired the best contemporary painters—his close friends the Pre-Raphaelites Dante Gabriel Rossetti, Ford Madox Brown, and chiefly Edward Burne-Jones—to design stained glass windows in their distinctive style. In doing so, while he adhered to medieval techniques, Morris broke away from traditional ecclesiastical stained glass styles and opened the way, albeit unknowingly, for the radical changes that were to come in the twentieth century.

Detail, St. Cecilia. *Second Presbyterian Church, 1936 South Michigan Avenue. Edward Burne-Jones and William Morris. Late 19th or early 20th century.*

New Directions in Stained Glass

Toward the close of the nineteenth century stained glass, heretofore almost exclusively an ecclesiastical art, suddenly veered into the secular sphere. Some of the impetus for this move had already begun with Morris and the Pre-Raphaelites who had designed stained glass windows of idealized medieval romances and legends for the homes of their wealthy clients.

Simultaneously, in Belgium, architect Victor Horta, one of the pioneers of Art Nouveau, incorporated stained glass into the flowing lines of his Solvay and Eetvelde residences in Brussels, as did Antonio Gaudi for the Güell Colony buildings near Barcelona, and Charles Rennie Mackintosh for the Willow Tearooms in Glasgow.

In the United States, Louis Comfort Tiffany designed hundreds of scenic windows for public buildings, the palatial residences of his fabulously wealthy clients and, always the innovator, for churches as well. Meanwhile, in Chicago, architects Louis H. Sullivan and Frank Lloyd Wright were using stained glass as a structural and ornamental material—Sullivan in the Auditorium Theatre Building and Wright in his Prairie houses.

While these exciting developments were taking place on both sides of the Atlantic, traditionalists Christopher Whall in England and Charles J. Connick of Boston were producing ecclesiastical stained glass windows in the manner of the twelfth and thirteenth centuries for new churches being built in the Gothic style. Although Whall and Connick did much to restore to the craft sound workmanship and the use of the best materials, as Morris had done, their work, however fine, could not reverse the trend toward modern art and architecture.

By the 1940s new methods of building construction made it possible to install whole shimmering walls of glass supported only by slender concrete or metal frames. At the same time, new materials like slab glass and epoxy resins, as well as new techniques like fused glass and glass appliqué eliminated even the need for leading.

These innovations and the availability of hundreds of ready-made colored and textured glasses have presented designers and craftsmen with a diversity of artistic opportunities undreamt of in the Middle Ages. Equally important has been the influence of the French abstract and expressionist painters Matisse, Leger, Braque, Rouault, and Chagall whose magnificent stained glass windows have brought fresh vision and renewed vitality to the age-old art.

Matisse, who spent most of his life studying the effect of light upon color, created for the Chapel of the Rosary at Vence, his last major work, what many consider the most luminous stained glass windows of the twentieth century. Based on the deceptively simple foliate designs of his paper collages, his windows in singing yellow, blue, and green flood the "chaste white chapel" with radiant color.

Another masterpiece, one of the first to be constructed entirely of slab glass set in concrete, was Leger's monumental frieze in brilliant colors banding three sides of the Church of the Sacred Heart at Audincourt. Abandoning the iconography of modern machinery and machine-like figures which distinguish his paintings, Leger here created large abstract tubular forms interspersed with symbols of peace and Christianity.

In Germany after World War II, the construction of hundreds of new churches and public buildings gave its artists, working in collaboration with distinguished architects, the incentive to break with the tragic past and to begin anew with baffling iconographies and strange organic forms that defy interpretation, but excite and challenge the imagination as stained glass has never done before.

For example, George Meistermann's spectacular window at St. Mary Church in Cologne invites and yet resists interpretation, suggesting rippling water on a pond, the swift movement of clouds, and the gathering of a summer storm. William Buschulte's window at St. Ursula Church in the same city may be a series of irregular overlapping crosses or, perhaps by another stretch of the imagination, a wraith-like Tree of Jesse.

Cloister window. Aachen Cathedral, Germany. Ludwig Schaffrath, mid-20th century. Note: Photographed from Stained Glass *by Lee Lawrence, et. al. Crown Publishers, 1976.*

Probably the greatest influence on contemporary stained glass design has been Ludwig Schaffrath. Composed of interpenetrating ribbons of glass expressive of constant motion, as in his window for the swimming pool at Ubach-Palenbach, or of mysterious amorphic shapes controlled by leadlines of varying thicknesses, as in his cloister window at Aachen Cathedral, Schaffrath's works convey an unforgettable mystic quality.

Although they use modern materials and techniques in highly original ways, the German artists have returned to the basics of stained glass art—pure color and graphic leadlines.

Since the 1950s American stained glass artists, showing a special affinity for the contemporary scene, have produced some of the most imaginative and diverse works of the twentieth century. For instance, Rodney Winfield's window at St. Peter and Paul Cathedral in Washington, D.C., a semi-abstract design set in modified Gothic traceries, suggests the path of flight in outer space and is designed to hold a chip of moon rock brought back to earth by astronauts Neil Armstrong and Edwin Aldrin.

For the spectacular slab glass mural at KLM's airline office in New York City, Gyorgy Kepes constructed a system of aluminum screens perforated with thousands of small openings. Over these, pieces of colored glass were fixed with clear epoxy and backlighted with a barrage of lights timed to blink at alternating intervals, giving the effect of night flight over a large city.

An unusual subject for a stained glass window, reflecting the modern age of technology, appears in a work created by Charles Z. Lawrence of the Willett Studios for the reception room of the Gore Manufacturing Company, a textile firm in Cherry Hill, Maryland. Inspired by a 3000X photomicrograph of textile fibers and the spaces between them magnified thousands of times, Lawrence translated what he saw into a gorgeous, sweeping stained glass fantasy of line and color.

Over the last quarter century a younger generation of artists on the West Coast—Cathy Stackpole Bunnell, Paul Marioni, and Robert Kehlmann, to name but a few—have introduced an entirely new concept, stained glass as an autonomous art, freed from the restrictions of architecture. As Kehlmann explains:"There is no reason why stained glass should have any limitations beyond those dictated by materials and a sensitivity to design. The traditional approach to stained glass as 'the handmaiden to architecture,' has forced many designers to feel the need to restrict or architecturally justify their work—even when making 'non-architectural' panels. It has impeded a healthy and creative exploration of the medium."[6]

While it is doubtful that stained glass can ever be divorced completely from architecture, the new direction, added to all the other innovations which have occurred with such astonishing rapidity since the early part of this century, brings yet another dimension to this age-old art which continues to grow and to promise exciting developments for the future.

Reception room window. Gore Manufacturing Co., Cherry Hill, Maryland. Charles Z. Lawrence of the Willett Stained Glass Studios, 1978.

Stained Glass by Chicago Glassmen

Clerestory wheel window.
Holy Family Church, 1080
West Roosevelt Road. Artist
unknown, c. 1860.
Diameter, 5 feet.

Chapter Two

It is doubtful that any city in the United States used stained glass more lavishly than Chicago did during the period from the Great Fire of 1871 to the Great Depression of the 1930s. Within this span of sixty years, which saw the rise and fall of Chicago as a major art glass center, Chicago glassmen produced thousands of shimmering decorations of outstanding artistry and craftsmanship for churches and synagogues, the palatial mansions of millionaires, the modest dwellings of the middle class, schools, libraries, hotels, theaters, restaurants, private clubs, railroad stations, and even railroad cars.

This extravagant use of glass was the direct result of the stained glass revival which emanated from England and France in the mid-nineteenth century and spread rapidly to the United States. In Chicago, however, the revival took on greater proportions because of the tremendous post-Fire population and building explosions which generated an enormous demand for ecclesiastical and secular stained glass art that lasted well into the 1920s.

The Great Depression and the Second World War brought building construction to a virtual standstill and forced most of the stained glass studios out of business. Moreover, when construction resumed after the war, the International style of architecture, which still dominates the city, shunned stained glass entirely for the "all-glass-skin" building. These were grievous blows from which the once flourishing industry is only now beginning to show signs of recovery.

Top of east facade window. First Baptist Congregational Church, 60 North Ashland Avenue. Geo. A. Misch & Bro., 1869. Width, 20 feet.

Although Chicago is no longer an important working center for stained glass, it is a vast living museum of the art housing inestimable treasures which Chicagoans, aware of their heritage, are conserving as one of their richest cultural legacies.

Beginnings and Growth

The earliest stained glass establishments in Chicago, all pre-dating the Great Fire, were: the W. H. Carse & Co. and Otto Jevne & Co. (1850s); Geo. A. Misch & Bro. (1864); and the W. H. Wells & Co. (1870). These firms designed and executed only religious windows, principally for the tall, narrow lancets of the Neo-Gothic churches then in vogue and springing up by the score throughout the central city and outlying neighborhoods.

Although Otto Jevne and George Misch did design pictorial windows of biblical themes, most of the windows were purely ornamental. For example, the six wheel windows in the lofty clerestory at Holy Family Church (1857-60), the oldest known stained glass windows in the city, are composed of circles within circles intersected by radiating spokes each containing a highly stylized floriate pattern.

Generally, however, most of the earliest windows consisted of a simple latticework of diamonds or squares of amber glass framed in narrow borders of brightly colored conventionalized flowers and vines. This type of window can be seen at the First Baptist Congregational Church (1869), the Trinity Episcopal Church (1873), and the Olivet Baptist Church (1875). The windows at the First Baptist Congregational Church were supplied by Geo. A. Misch, and those at the Trinity Episcopal Church were executed by the Wells Company. The windows in other early churches cannot be identified. All, however, are of the finest craftsmanship, and many are in pristine condition.

After the holocaust, the growth of the stained glass business, like that of the city itself, was phenomenal. In the decade between 1880 and 1890 when Chicago's population neared 750,000 there were more than a dozen shops; by 1900 at least twenty; and by 1910 when the population soared to over 2,185,000 more than fifty. These ranged from small arts and crafts studios employing one or two craftsmen to the Munich Studio with thirty-five; the John J. Kinsella Co. and McCully & Miles with about fifty; and Flanagan & Biedenweg, the giant of them all, with an estimated one hundred.

In addition to these firms, others of equal importance whose works, like the aforementioned, still exist and can be identified were: Healy & Millet; the Linden Glass Co.; the Temple Art Glass Co.; the studio of Thomas Augustin O'Shaughnessy; Giannini & Hilgart; and the Drehobl Bros. Art Glass Co. Of these, and all the other firms which did business sometime during Chicago's stained glass heyday, only Giannini & Hilgart (under different management) and the Drehobl Bros. Art Glass Co. (under the same family management) are in operation today.

The Glassmen

The majority of the glassmen were foreign-born, of English, French, German or Irish descent. Like thousands of other immigrants they came to booming Chicago to escape oppressive governments or to seek better economic opportunities. Most had been trained in some phase of the craft in their native countries, but the preponderance of skilled artisans were the Germans, who so dominated the field by the 1880s that some knowledge of their language was almost a prerequisite for securing a job.

Not infrequently, after working for established local firms, the Germans organized their own companies, or joined in partnerships with versatile American artists and designers who had a natural aptitude for the art. For example, Ernest J. Spierling, a skilled German artisan who had been employed by several local firms, joined Frank L. Linden in 1882 to form Spierling & Linden (later the Linden Glass Co.). Linden, a Rockford, Illinois fresco painter and designer had worked for several New York City interior decorating concerns before moving to Chicago.

Vestibule window. Trinity Episcopal Church, 125 East 26th Street. W. H. Wells Co., 1872-73. Width, 5 feet.

Joseph E. Flanagan, formerly a manager for Geo. A. Misch & Bro. and McCully & Miles, left the latter in 1885 to organize with William C. Biedenweg, a German designer-craftsman, Flanagan & Biedenweg, which in turn would launch at least three other important firms. Flanagan, a seminal figure in the development of Chicago's stained glass trade, was already an experienced glassman before settling in Chicago, having served apprenticeships with several Midwest establishments, the first in New Albany, Indiana, his hometown, at the age of twelve.

Fritz Hilgart, a German glass cutter, and Cincinnati sculptor and designer Orlando Giannini, a former manager of the Cincinnati Art Pottery Co., organized Giannini & Hilgart in 1899. Max Guler, a china and glass painter from the region of Munich, Germany, L. Holzchuh, a bookkeeper, and Dennis S. Shanahan, formerly a salesman for Flanagan & Biedenweg, founded the Munich Studio in 1903.

In the same year, Henry J. Niethart and Joseph E. Vogel, a glass cutter who had been a foreman for Flanagan & Biedenweg, founded the Temple Art Glass Co. Like Frank Linden and Orlando Giannini, Vogel worked on various art glass projects for Frank Lloyd Wright and a number of other prominent Prairie School architects. The last company to enter the field was the Drehobl Bros. Art Glass Co., organized by Frank J. Drehobl, previously a glass cutter for Flanagan & Biedenweg, and his brother Joseph in 1919.

The American partners George L. Healy and Louis J. Millet, and Thomas Augustin O'Shaughnessy, an independent artist, in addition to their expertise in stained glass, were all exceptionally well-schooled in the fine and decorative arts. Healy, the son of G.P.A. Healy, the well-known Chicago portrait painter, and Millet, a native of New York City, had met while studying architecture and decoration at L'Ecole des Beaux Arts in Paris. After completing their courses at that prestigious institution in 1879, they came to Chicago the following year and (encouraged, it is said, by their architect friend Louis H. Sullivan) opened an interior decorating establishment specializing in stained glass. Highly successful, they moved in 1884 to larger quarters in a two-story building on Wabash Avenue where their showroom, described by one visitor as a "veritable artist's den," displayed some of the most original art glass then being produced.

Thomas O'Shaughnessy, born in Medon, Missouri in 1870, is reputed to have made his first stained glass window at the age of twelve for the Chapel of the Sisters of Loretto Academy in Moberly, Missouri. Upon his graduation from the Fine Arts Academy in Kansas City, Missouri in 1894, O'Shaughnessy came to Chicago the same year. After setting up a studio for commercial art on North State Street, he enrolled at the Art Institute's School of Design where he took courses with Louis Millet, one of the founders of the school, and with Alphonse Mucha, the illustrious Czech artist of Art Nouveau poster fame.

Detail of O'Shaughnessy window on page 68.

After a visit to Ireland in 1900, O'Shaughnessy conceived the idea of transmuting Celtic ornamentation into stained glass, particularly motifs from the *Book of Kells,* which he had studied from the original folios at Trinity College in Dublin. To this purpose, he experimented for years to produce pot metal glass of a transparency that would reproduce the brilliant colors and luminous quality of the great medieval illuminated manuscript. Achieving his goal in 1911, he forsook a successful career in commercial art and at the age of forty-one went on to become one of America's finest ecclesiastical stained glass artists.

The Glass

With the exception of O'Shaughnessy, who used only his own patented pot metal glass made of extremely fine sands he discovered near Ottawa, Illinois and had processed at a Kokomo, Indiana glass factory, Chicago firms purchased domestic glass from Indiana, Ohio, Pennsylvania, New York, and West Virginia, and antique glass from France and Germany. Although it was considerably more expensive than domestic glass, some glassmen favored the imported product because of its greater color resonance and luminosity. The Linden Co., for instance, advertised that it used "only the finest imported glass," while the Munich Studio stressed the quality and beauty of its "exquisite antique glass of luminous unfading colors."

Nevertheless, and despite the claims of glassmen partial to French and German glass, American glass had by the 1880s improved dramatically. Hand-blown antique glass comparable to that produced in France and Germany became available and a wide range of new machine-made glasses appeared on the market.

Known as "cathedral glass," machine-made glasses were rolled into large textured or untextured sheets containing internal waves, streaks, or mottlings of contrasting or harmonizing colors. Novel effects could also be obtained by using embossed rollers to impress pebbled, rippled, or hammered textures on the surface of the glass while it was semi-molten.

Much cathedral glass was of the so-called "opalescent" variety. This was a purely American product invented by New York artists Louis Comfort Tiffany and John La Farge which would revolutionize the stained glass industry.

As developed by Tiffany and La Farge, the new glass techniques were described in detail in *Scribner's Monthly* of January, 1881. "The hot glass, while at red heat, is rolled with corrugated rollers, punched and pressed by various roughened tools, or is squeezed and pressed into corrugations by lateral pressure, or is stamped by dies. The 'bulls-eyes' produced in making sheet glass, by whirling it round on a rod while soft, are also cut into various shapes, or while still soft, are gently pressed into new shapes ... Next to this comes a revival and modification of the old Venetian method of imbedding bits of colored glass on the table on which plate glass is made, and then pouring the hot glass (either white or colored) over the table and rolling it down in the usual manner to press the colored threads or pieces into the sheet. New styles of opalescent glass, new methods of mixing colors in the glasshouse, have also been tried, and with many surprising and beautiful results. Lastly comes one of the most original features of all, and this is the use of solid masses and lumps of glass pressed while hot into moulds, giving a great number of facets like a cut stone, or by taking blocks of glass and roughly chipping them into small faces. These when set into the window, have all the effects of the most brilliant gems, changing their shade of color with every changing angle of vision."[1]

Although it was Tiffany who popularized opalescent glass in America, it was Healy & Millet and La Farge who first introduced it to Europe. At the Paris Exposition of 1889 their displays caused a sensation. In fact, the new American glasses so impressed the French Government that it purchased several of Healy & Millet's "remarkable collection of small panels" for the Musée des Arts Décoratifs in Paris.

Writing in the *Revue des Arts Décoratifs,* Edouard Didron, the French glass designer, vividly described these: "These pieces are skillfully designed to seduce the eye; interlaces in the Byzantine style, intricate and most delicately formed and yellow in color, separated by straight leads from a white background that has an onyx appearance; scrollwork branching into green palm leaves with red fruits; Persian stained-glass windows in vivid and varied hues resembling translucent carpets; garlands in gray stones on a white background studded with large gold cabochons. All of these ornamentations certainly provide unforeseen effects and have marked originality, although inspired by Oriental art. There is a pearly glass with reflections of olive, yellow, green, and reds, colored with a power unknown until now and most arresting to see; it suggests pearly transparent marble, or at times thick sheets of horn, that encloses precious stones and glittering spangles. Cut into narrow strips with rough surfaces catching the light, or in minuscule fragments that seem to sparkle with a rare intensity. American glass is a superb material and brings to our windows a precious element."[2]

But the most spectacular display of the new glasses was in Chicago at the World's Columbian Exposition of 1893, where displays by Flanagan & Biedenweg, Healy & Millet, McCully & Miles, the W. H. Wells Co., and Tiffany's resplendent chapel showed the almost unlimited artistic possibilities of this versatile and purely American product.

Styles of Glass

Actually, Chicago firms had been using the new glasses for a wide range of domestic purposes since their inception. Noting this trend, the *Inland Architect and Builder,* a Chicago periodical widely read throughout the Midwest, reported in May, 1882 that "scarcely a home of any architectural pretension can be found that does not have stained glass in door or window and even fire screen ..." So great was the demand for the art that only two years later the same publication stated that "even the humble household has its brightly tinted window ..." Known as "Victorian" glass, these decorations made no pretension to great art, but were generally well-crafted and of good design.

Victorian windows were of two general types. One incorporated naturalistic studies of roses, morning glories, or poppies leaded into clear glass bordered with small panes of squares or diamonds in which were set cabochons or opalescent glass jewels. A popular variation, one of several combining clear and colored glass, featured a centered rondel or large faceted jewel from which leadlines radiated through clear glass to give the impression of a dazzling sunburst.

The other type consisted of flattened conventionalized flower studies derived from the botanical drawings of the mid-nineteenth century Englishmen Owen Jones in his *Grammar of Ornament* and Christopher Dresser in his *Principles of Decorative Design.* These windows were made entirely of colored glass in which were set abstract designs of fleur-de-lis, tulips, or lilies surrounded by convoluting leaves and petals harmonizing with and growing out of the central theme.

Victorian windows were made by the thousands not only for decoration but also for the practical purpose, as Flanagan & Biedenweg advertised, of "blocking out the ugly sights of alleys and close by buildings." Most were made for the residences and apartment buildings of the middle and upper class in Hyde Park-Kenwood, Wicker Park, Logan Square, Old and New Towns, and the Jackson Boulevard landmark district where they can still be seen by the score.

When Art Nouveau, a rage in Paris at the turn of the century, became the fashion, Chicago firms were quick to make their own adaptations of the avant-garde style. A Flanagan & Biedenweg advertisement of 1900, for example, showed one panel of lilies with undulating leaves and stems, a favorite motif of Paris practitioners of the style, and another of a lissome mermaid with long, flowing hair in the manner of the poster art of Eugene Grasset and Alphonse Mucha. Art Nouveau panels were made by most firms until about 1915 when the style was no longer in fashion.

While Victorian and Art Nouveau styles were in the ascendancy, Frank Lloyd Wright had already created a radically new kind of art glass for his Prairie houses. Angular, and "absolutely in the flat," Wright's early designs were based on conventionalized flowers and plants; later ones were severely abstract, but all were planned to thoroughly integrate with his "organic" architecture.

Typically, Wright used little stained glass, preferring instead clear glass set with small pieces of colored glass to permit unobstructed nature views. As he explained: "Nothing is more annoying to me than any tendency toward realism of form in window-glass, to get mixed up with the view outside."[3] Arranged in continuous horizontal bands across entire walls, the windows were structural elements of his architecture and at the same time shimmering glass curtain screens providing privacy.

Wright often complained that his art glass was unappreciated, but that was hardly the case, for such eminent Prairie School architects as George Grant Elmslie, George W. Maher, Walter Burley Griffin, and William E. Drummond modeled their designs after his, and by the 1920s when Wright had abandoned stained glass for clear sheet glass, local firms had long since adopted his designs as their own.

Although Wright's windows can be appreciated in single units owned by major museums, including Chicago's Art Institute, they are best seen *in situ* in such important buildings as the Robie House and Unity Temple where they show how carefully Wright planned his designs to create an integrated environment.

Stained Glass for the Wealthy

That the city's most affluent citizens were just as much enamored of stained glass as the middle class was proved by an article which appeared in 1896 in *Art for America,* a Chicago publication. It stated that "the old notion of the incapacity of Chicago artists engaged in the production of art glass is rapidly dying out and the wealthy and refined of our city are now honoring their artistic creations by placing them in their residences and employing glass decorations profusely to embellish their homes."[4] While the publication was correct in its pronouncement, it was nearly two decades behind the times in its assessment, for local firms had been decorating the grand mansions of the wealthy since the late 1870s.

Living room windows. Robie House, 5757 South Woodlawn Avenue. Designed by Frank Lloyd Wright, executed by the Linden Glass Co., 1909. Width, 30 inches each.

McCully & Miles, for example, made a specialty of providing stained glass decorations for the wealthy, advertising consistently to an exclusive clientele in Chicago's *Elite Directory and Club List*. Healy & Millet also catered to the monied elite, as did Mitchel & Halbach, among whose affluent clients were industrialist Richard T. Crane, meat packer Philip D. Armour, brewer Conrad Seipp, and department store magnate Marshall Field. Of the Linden Glass Co. it was said that for their best work "one must go upon Prairie and Calumet avenues, and along the Lake drive." Yet except for an occasional old and faded photograph in which one faintly discerns a stained glass window above a fireplace mantel, or decorative panels used as room dividers, we have no way of knowing what such decorations looked like, since most of the stained glass was destroyed or vanished when the mansions they adorned were demolished.

The Pullman Palace Car

A reflection of the opulence of the time was the Pullman palace car, whose inventor George M. Pullman reasoned that if stained glass was such an important decorative element in the homes of wealthy Americans, why should they not enjoy the art when they traveled? Accordingly, he set aside space in his vast southside railroad plant for a stained glass workshop and hired German and Italian artisans to design and execute small Victorian stained glass transoms, door lights, and jeweled domes by the thousands for his sumptuous rolling stock, replete with crystal chandeliers, plush carpeting, glowing dark mahogany woodwork, and rich damask upholstery.

Stairway landing window. Piper Hall, Mundelein College of Loyola University Chicago, 6363 Sheridan Road. Artist unknown, 1909. Width, 7 feet.

Pullman was looked upon with disdain by the "tastemakers" of his time, who considered his invention vulgar and gaudy. Pullman himself, however, thought otherwise. "I have always held," he moralized, "that people are greatly influenced by their physical surroundings. Take the roughest man, a man whose lines have brought him into the coarsest and poorest surroundings, and bring him into a room elegantly carpeted and finished, and the effect upon his bearing is immediate. The more artistic and refined the external surroundings, the better and more refined the man."[5]

While Pullman's stained glass and other decorations made no great artistic contribution to American art or culture, his cars were unabashedly admired by the public as well as by American industrialists and foreign potentates who purchased customized Pullman cars to ride the rails with all the comforts and luxurious appointments to which they were accustomed.

Stained Glass in Public Buildings

Just when stained glass began to be used in Chicago's public buildings is difficult to say, for little or no glass art appears in photographs of pre-Fire hotels, theaters, retail establishments, or civic buildings, and colored glass is rarely mentioned in books about Chicago's earliest architecture. About the closest ornamentation to stained glass was the vast quantity of clear beveled glass provided by James Berry & Co. for the windows of architect William W. Boyington's palatial one-block square Grand Pacific Hotel, imitative of the Louvre in Paris.

The Great Fire of 1871 completely consumed the splendid structure just a few days before it was to have opened. Undaunted, the management rebuilt it within the year on the same site and according to Boyington's original plan. In the bar room where La Salle Street traders gathered was a lofty clear glass window richly bordered with an exuberant floral design of colored glass.

Stained glass was more conspicuous in architect Dankmar Adler's 1879 Central Music Hall where tall, round-arched windows of an intricate floral-geometric pattern swept upwards from the ground floor to the high second-floor balcony, diffusing a soft light throughout the vast hall.

Skylight panel of Auditorium Theatre. Roosevelt University, Michigan Avenue at Congress Street. Designed by Louis H. Sullivan, executed by Healy & Millet, 1889. Width, 33 inches.

By 1884 stained glass had become such an important decorative element in public structures that when the new Board of Trade building neared completion that year, it was decided to conduct a nationwide competition to select themes for the large lunettes in the great trading room. Five of the twenty entrants were Chicagoans. Among them was George Misch, who submitted watercolors of modern steam-driven reapers, mowers, and corn-shellers against a background of wheat and corn fields. McCully & Miles's designs featured circular medallions picturing scenes of agriculture and industry framed in rich mosaic glass borders. Healy & Millet's drawings depicted heroic figures of sculptors, hewers of wood, and blacksmiths representing the pioneers who had built the great new city. Although these entries were seriously considered by the judges, it was John La Farge's studies of life-sized goddesses symbolic of the bounties of agriculture that won the commission.

The most lavish use of glass art in a public building was in Adler & Sullivan's world-famous Auditorium Hotel and Theatre, now Roosevelt University, completed in 1889. One of the world's greatest architectural ornamentalists, Sullivan's philosophy of decoration was that it should be "organic, growing out of the mass rather than being applied to it." Applying his concept to the Auditorium, he explained: "A single idea or principle is taken as the basis of the color scheme, that is to say, use is made of but one color in each instance, and that color is associated with gold ... The stained glass, of which a moderate use is made, is carefully harmonized with the prevailing tone of

color in the decoration."[6] It is difficult to understand why Sullivan understated his use of stained glass, for it appeared in an amazing variety of his own designs throughout the building.

The Auditorium windows, as well as those in other buildings designed by Sullivan, were executed by his long-time friend and associate Louis Millet, whose philosophy of ornamentation matched his own and upon whom Sullivan, by his own admission, depended for the realization of his designs and colors.

In the sedate hotel lobby of rich, tawny marble were large lunettes containing Sullivanesque arabesques in amber on a background of gold bordered by glowing jewels, variations of which appeared in the mezzanine windows and skylight. In the north staircase each landing had large rectangular windows, some filled with a design of intersecting ellipses of pale gold, others with a repeating daisy pattern of greenish gold and brown.

Overhead in the foyer of the small banquet room, now Ganz Hall, electric light bulbs were hidden by opaque white glass panels over which were placed perforated metal grilles of a stylized foliate design, each bordered by an angular strapwork pattern of white glass against a ground of brownish gold. In the west wall, a series of light screens in pale green featured gold scrolls highlighted with small cabochons of light blue, amber, and gold. The banquet room itself had twelve lunettes of a centralized magnolia-like flower with spiraling tendrils. In the great arched ceiling of the immense main dining room were skylight panels each containing a floral pattern of pale green and rose in a background of light gold.

The magnificent auditorium had a basic color scheme of rich ivory and gold and skylight panels of ivory colored glass inset with a design of Celtic knots in deep amber against a pale amber ground. The only pictorial windows in the building were the heads of three muses symbolizing the theatrical arts which appeared in the lunettes above the theater's vestibule doors.

A surprising number of these splendid windows, now almost a century old, are still in place and intact, revealing yet another facet of Sullivan's fertile imagination and his genius for ornamentation.

A year after the Auditorium opened, architect Solon S. Beman's monumental Grand Central Station began operations. The huge waiting room featured nine large windows topped by lunettes of amber and blue textured cathedral glass, selected by the architect because "it gave good effects from both sides."

The Chicago Stock Exchange Building, another Adler & Sullivan masterpiece, was completed in 1894. Around the periphery of the trading room stenciled with magnificent Sullivanesque designs was a skylight filled with over two hundred art glass panels inset with a design of hexagons. When the building

Above right:
Detail of skylight, foyer of Ganz Hall. Roosevelt University, Michigan Avenue at Congress Street. Designed by Louis H. Sullivan, executed by Healy & Millet, 1889. Width, approx. 2½ feet.

Below:
Skylight panels of the trading room, Chicago Stock Exchange. Now in the Art Institute, Michigan Avenue at Adams Street. Designed by Louis H. Sullivan, executed by Healy & Millet, 1894.

was dismantled in 1971, the panels, painted and boarded over, were discovered and salvaged. Later, in 1977, after being restored, they were installed in their original setting in the reconstructed trading room at the Art Institute.

The Fisher Building, an eighteen-story skyscraper completed in 1896, had a vaulted ceiling of mosaic glass and in the vestibule doors large, ornamental fish etched in clear glass. The marine theme continued in the wall light fixtures which displayed playful dolphins leaded in orange and green cathedral glass. It is thought that all these decorations were the work of Healy & Millet.

About the last of the "tall buildings" to have stained glass art was Holabird & Roche's 1905-09 Republic Building (demolished in 1961). The lobby of white marble was embellished with panels of opaque white glass containing a pale blue abstract floral design akin to those of the Prairie School style.

The Strike and Standardization

Although the demand for domestic as well as ecclesiastical art glass had continued to increase through the 1890s, by 1900 the Chicago stained glass industry was besieged with problems caused by intense competition among local firms and by competitors from the eastern states and Europe. Glassmen worked twelve to fifteen hours a day and full time on Saturdays to finish large commissions but were often summarily dismissed when the jobs were completed. Moreover, owners were accused of laying off older, higher paid personnel and replacing them with inexperienced apprentices to cut costs.

Finally, unrest among employees led them in 1900 to form the Amalgamated Glass Workers Association, Local I. In 1903 shop owners countered with their own organization, the National Glass Manufacturers Association, now the Stained Glass Association of America, of which Joseph Flanagan was elected the first president.

In 1905, after a few brief walkouts, a full-fledged strike of 650 union members ensued. The strike lasted well into 1907 and was finally terminated with a union contract that provided fixed hours and better employment stability. But the disruptive force of the strike saw union membership dwindle to less than 100, while proprietors faced the grim reality of German firms taking a large part of the business.

Problems between labor and management still existed, and Flanagan felt that the tensions between them could be eased if the issues could be discussed openly and then published in a periodical. Out of the subsequent meetings was born *The Ornamental Glass Bulletin* (now *Stained Glass* magazine). Filled with articles on all aspects of the art, the journal played an important role in establishing mutual understanding between artists, craftsmen, and management. Flanagan became its editor in 1908, a post he held until his death in 1928.

In an attempt to overcome the vexing problem of price-cutting, Flanagan, Frank Linden, and Max Mueller of Schuler & Mueller decided in 1909 to publish *The International Art Glass Catalogue.* To launch it each association member was asked to submit twenty window designs of standard sizes to determine average prices to which all members could adhere. The profusely illustrated catalogue was mailed to architects, millwork supply houses, and builders. Published until 1915, it clearly reflected the extreme pressure on all firms to produce stained glass decorations as cheaply as possible. Among the illustrations were stilted landscapes, renditions of fuzzy cats and shaggy dogs, and vulgarized presentations of Art Nouveau.

A complete standardization of the industry, however, then as now, could never be realized, for stained glass is an art which demands the closest collaboration between the artist and the craftsman. One needs only to be reminded, for example, of the inspired partnerships of Burne-Jones and William Morris, Sullivan and Millet, and in modern times Marc Chagall and Charles Marq.

Ecclesiastical Stained Glass

One of the clearest indications of Chicago's astonishing growth after the Great Fire was the large number of ecclesiastical structures that were built to serve the religious needs of the European immigrants who came to live in the city's burgeoning ethnic neighborhoods. By 1910 it is estimated that Chicago had between twelve and thirteen hundred houses of worship and by 1930 nearly two thousand, a figure that remains substantially the same today. Excluding a few in the International style, virtually all of these churches have stained glass windows, many of them equal to the finest in Europe.

To make a selection of ecclesiastical stained glass for this book from so vast a field was a difficult task indeed, for almost every exploration would reveal another treasure. However, we have tried to present as many styles and techniques of stained glass as possible within the artistic and historical context of the preceding pages. All are splendid examples, though by no means the only ones, of what can be found in houses of worship throughout the city.

Victorian Style Windows

Victorian style windows with simple geometric-floral patterns frequently appear in old Chicago churches. These were less expensive than figural or landscape windows, an important consideration for congregations with limited budgets.

The La Salle Street Church (1882-86) has five tall, double-lancet Victorian windows on either side of the nave. Each has delightful designs of flowers, leaves, and trinity symbols. The beautiful *Good Shepherd* window in the east facade, one of the few Victorian windows with religious subject matter, has a small panel of Jesus carrying a lamb on his shoulders surrounded by a joyous profusion of conventionalized flowers and vines set in Gothic traceries.

Left:

The Good Shepherd *window.*
LaSalle Street Church, 1136
North LaSalle Drive. Artist
unknown, 1886. Width, 18 feet.

Right:

West facade window.
The Greenstone Church, Pullman
United Methodist Church, 11211
South St. Lawrence Avenue.
Artist unknown, 1882. Width,
11 feet.

Another unusual ornamental window, though not strictly Victorian, is in the west facade of the Greenstone Church built in 1882 by George Pullman for his model industrial town. Twelve feet in diameter, it is a wheel window composed of leaded squares of white glass with radiating spokes in bright red, green, and yellow glass. Beneath the wheel are five small arched panels with colors and geometric patterns echoing those above.

The Lake View Presbyterian Church (1887-88) has on each side of the nave a charming arrangement of a stylized floral design in singing red, orange, blue, yellow, and green cathedral glass which alternates with another of naturalistic vines and leaves in amber, green, and gold.

The Church of Our Saviour (1888-89) in addition to five windows of religious subjects by Tiffany, houses a colorful display of Victorian lights on each side of the nave, in the clerestory, and in the south facade. Behind the altar is a spectacular Victorian window displaying a large daisy-like flower surrounded by radiating petals with shimmering impressed cabochons.

Left:

East facade windows. Lake View Presbyterian Church, 716 West Addison Street. Artist unknown, 1889. Width, c. 12½ feet.

Right:

Chancel window. Church of Our Saviour, 530 West Fullerton Parkway. Artist unknown, 1889. Width, 6½ feet.

Munich Style Art Glass

The most popular and prevalent stained glass windows in Chicago churches are the so-called "Munich" windows, which can be seen by the hundreds in churches that once had large German, Bohemian, Lithuanian, Polish, and Ukrainian congregations.

A master of the style was Max Guler, who founded the Munich Studio in Chicago in 1903. Guler had studied painting in Munich, Germany and, not surprisingly, his work shows the influence of the German Baroque style in his use of elaborate ornamentation, asymmetrical figure groupings, strong contrasts between light and shadow, and abundant architectural detail.

Splendid examples of Guler's art can be seen in the windows at SS. Cyril and Methodius Church (1913) built for a Bohemian congregation. Most of the windows present biblical scenes, but some express the parishioners' strong religious ties to their native country. Among the latter are SS. Cyril and Methodius bringing the church to the Slavic people; St. Ludmilla and her young grandson Wenceslaus; St. Wenceslaus ruler of Bohemia; and the baptism of Borivoj, Bohemia's first Christian duke.

Presentation of Christ in the Temple. *SS. Cyril and Methodius Church, 5009 South Hermitage Avenue. Max Guler of the Munich Studio, Chicago, 1913. Width, 8 feet. The church has since closed.*

A fine example of Guler's art is *The Presentation of Christ in the Temple.* The principal figures in this window are the Virgin Mary robed in shimmering light gold and the slumbering Christ Child wrapped in white swaddling clothes. Subordinate and in contrast to them are Simeon, Joseph, and Anna cloaked in heavy mantles of somber brown, gray, and blue. The asymmetrical figure groupings—Mary and Joseph to the left, Simeon, Anna, and the child to the right—are adroitly balanced and joined by Mary's outstretched arms and the large palm branch, a symbol of rejoicing, held by a child.

Guler's predilection for detailed architectural ornament can be seen in the menorah deeply carved into the massive rectangular post, the egg and dart and Greek key design on the lintel behind Mary and Joseph, the deep shadows on the variegated marble floor, and the ornate decoration in the arched border of simulated marble which frames the entire composition. Although the window is heavily painted with dark oxides, as most of Guler's are, the glass retains its luminosity because of his masterful brushwork.

Sullivan's Art Glass at K.A.M. Temple

Adler & Sullivan's synagogue masterpiece K.A.M. Temple (1890-91), now the Pilgrim Baptist Church, was originally erected for Chicago's oldest Jewish congregation. Adler's father, incidentally, had been the rabbi from 1861 to 1883. This impressive structure resembles the Auditorium Building which the partners had just completed. The interior, in addition to splendid stencils and plasterwork by Sullivan, has exquisite stained glass windows in a basic color scheme of lavender, gold, and amber brown designed by the architect and executed by Healy & Millet in deeply rippled cathedral glass.

The rectangular windows in the spacious auditorium each repeat a delicate lavender star of David entwined in a Sullivanesque arabesque highlighted with smooth, reddish orange cabochons. On either side of the vestibule are small lights with variations of the auditorium arabesque. The large lunettes in the balcony are divided into arcs of interweaving knot designs similar to those in Celtic ornamentation.

Healy & Millet and McCully & Miles

The Second Presbyterian Church (1872-74), a formidable English Neo-Gothic edifice erected for the millionaires whose palatial mansions graced nearby Prairie, Indiana, and Calumet avenues, contains a veritable gallery of stained glass art. Fourteen windows are by Louis Comfort Tiffany; one is by John La Farge; two by Burne-Jones and William Morris (all to be discussed later); one is by Healy & Millet; and four by McCully & Miles.

Healy & Millet's *Cast Thy Garment About Thee and Follow Me,* installed in 1895, is, as far as we know, the only extant religious window in Chicago by the firm. It depicts the drama of St. Peter's release from prison by an angel. The poignant scene is made memorable by the artist's unusually sensitive portrayal of the saint still doubtful of his freedom and the angel who reassures him. Paramount to the composition are the sweeping contours of the figures' robes, which were achieved by outlining long, narrow strips of rippled opalescent glass with leading. The same glass cut with and against the grain shapes the cypress trees and other nature forms in the background.

Above right:

Auditorium windows. Pilgrim Baptist Church, formerly K.A.M. Temple, 3301 South Indiana Avenue. Designed by Louis H. Sullivan, executed by Healy & Millet, 1891. Width, 40 inches.

Below:

Detail, Cast Thy Garment About Thee and Follow Me. *Second Presbyterian Church, 1936 South Michigan Avenue. Healy & Millet, c. 1895. Full width, 9 feet.*

McCully & Miles's *Beside the Still Waters* and the untitled triptych beneath it, designed by an unknown artist, present simple pastoral scenes in various shades of green. Pebbled glass causes the illusion of flickering lights on the clear pools of water and the verdant foliage of the trees. Chicago was deep into the Arts and Crafts Movement when these windows were installed in 1910 and they are exceptionally fine examples of that style.

Noteworthy also are the charming, stylized pomegranate designs in the windows at floor level on both sides of the nave and also those in the reception room doors. All of these were designed by Howard Van Doren Shaw, a prominent Chicago architect and a member of the church who reconstructed the formerly Neo-Gothic nave in the Arts and Crafts style after it had been destroyed by a fire in 1900.

Flanagan & Biedenweg

Although Flanagan & Biedenweg was Chicago's largest stained glass company, only a handful of its art glass windows can be positively identified today: two large occhio windows at St. Vincent de Paul Church (1895-97) and a panel from the *Magi Window,* presently not *in situ,* donated to De Paul University by Joseph Flanagan.

East transept window. St. Vincent de Paul Church, 1010 West Webster Avenue. Flanagan & Biedenweg, c. 1897. Width, 22 feet.

The occhio in the east transept at St. Vincent de Paul centers upon Christ enthroned as King, the one in the west transept upon St. Vincent de Paul, founder of the Vincentian Order. Both windows are composed of antique glass masterfully painted in the Italian Renaissance style. The east occhio, rich in reds and blues, is especially radiant in the morning light; in the afternoon it is quiet and awe-inspiring. Conversely, the west occhio in yellow, orange, and amber is quiet in the morning light, but intensely bright and active by mid-afternoon.

The panel of the *Magi Window,* a magnificent work, won the Grand Prize for American glass at the St. Louis World's Fair of 1904. The expressions of adoration on the faces of the three kings are matched by the wondrous gifts which they bear and by their robes which are encrusted with precious jewels. The window, flawlessly balanced in color and composition, is made entirely of opalescent glass.

Frank Lloyd Wright's Designs

Far removed from traditional subjects and designs in ecclesiastical stained glass art are Frank Lloyd Wright's windows at Unity Temple in Oak Park, Illinois constructed between 1906 and 1909. Wright conceived these windows as an integral part of the ornament and structure of the building and thought of the temple itself as a "Room in the service of Man for the worship of God."

The building, a massive block-like structure, scarcely suggests the ingenious interior lighting plan so vividly described by Wright in his *Autobiography*. "The large supporting posts," he writes, "were so set in plan as to form a double tier of alcoves on four sides of the room. I flooded these alcoves with light from above to get a sense of a happy cloudless day. And with this feeling for light the ceiling ... became skylight sifting through and between the intersecting concrete beams, filtering through amber ceiling lights. Thus managed the light would, rain or shine, have the warmth of sunlight. Artificial lighting took place there at night as well. This scheme of lighting was integral, gave diffusion and kept the room space clear."[7]

The twenty leaded clerestory windows in the alcoves stretch in a horizontal band around the room. Each repeats a highly abstract floral design of small pieces of subtly tinted yellow glass. As the light changes, the windows become shimmering ribbons of glass through which one sees trees, sun, and sky. The yellow, orange, and light brown glass in the twenty-five deeply recessed panels of the skylight, each containing the same blocky geometric pattern, casts a warm amber glow throughout the small but "noble room." A neo-plastic design—foreshadowing those later seen in paintings by Mondrian—in gray and white outlined by dark zinc cames decorates the long, slotted apertures in each of the four stairwell towers, a Wrightian solution to diffuse light into what otherwise would be dark areas.

Wright, a stickler for perfection, entrusted three firms to execute his meticulous designs: Giannini & Hilgart, the Linden Company, and the Temple Art Glass Company. The latter was chosen by the architect for the project at Unity Temple.

Glass door in passageway linking church and parish house. Unity Temple, 875 Lake Street, Oak Park, Illinois. Designed by Frank Lloyd Wright, executed by the Linden Glass Co., 1910. Width, 3½ feet.

65

Thomas O'Shaughnessy's Windows

St. Patrick's Church, Chicago's oldest religious building, was erected between 1852-56 for a predominantly Irish Catholic congregation. The church is noted for its splendid stained glass windows created by Thomas Augustin O'Shaughnessy when the church was redecorated in 1911.

A devout Irish Catholic and a lifetime student of Irish art and history, O'Shaughnessy chose for the twelve nave windows installed in 1912 studies of the Irish saints, scholars, and missionaries who played important roles in fostering faith and learning throughout Europe after the barbarian invasions. Among the subjects are: St. Patrick, Ireland's patron saint, preaching to the Celts and Picts in defiance of the Druid priests at the sacred hill of Tara; St. Attracta, the founder of Irish convents, about to accept the veil from St. Patrick; St. Brendan the voyager greeting Indians as he steps from his barque on the coast of America; and St. Brigid, Ireland's patroness of the arts, teaching in the schools she founded.

At the top and bottom of each window are exquisite borders of intricate, Celtic interlaces adopted from the *Book of Kells,* the inspiration for O'Shaughnessy's art. All the windows are made of O'Shaughnessy's own pot metal glass in delicate pastel shades of pink, yellow, blue, green, and mauve set off by an abundance of leaf green and pearly white.

In the balcony is the celebrated triptych of Faith, Hope, and Charity which O'Shaughnessy donated to the church in 1921 in honor of Terence McSwiney, the lord mayor of Cork who died in a hunger strike the previous year. It is composed of thousands of tiny pieces of mosaic glass fastened with hairline bronze cames. Except for the finest details, the artist used no paint. The impersonal, rigidly posed frontal figures of Hope and Charity act as sentinels guarding the center panel of Faith, a complex work of Irish iconography.

At the top of the Faith window, in the curve of its arch, is a large shamrock representing the Trinity. In the center of the shamrock the Eye of the Deity surveys a large Celtic cross which has angels within and around it. Integrated with the great cross, but subordinate to it, are Greek and Latin crosses symbolizing the universality of the Church. Bordering the horizontal and vertical members of the crosses are supplicating Art Nouveau angels gowned in satiny white tinged with pale pink, yellow, and blue. At the axis of the cross stands the serene figure of the Virgin Mary robed in radiant white, her halo of twelve stars lit by the setting sun.

Pictured in miniature within the great cross, in company with saints who appear life-size in the nave windows, are Duns Scotus the philosopher, St. Malachi the prophet, and St. Firgil the geographer. At the base of the cross, rising out of what O'Shaughnessy called the "lurid colors of purgatory," is the spirit of Terence McSwiney transported by angels through the golden ages of Irish learning and history. A complicated pattern of circles, spirals, and whorls embellishes the various themes and unifies the entire work.

Detail, the Faith *window. St. Patrick's Church, 718 West Adams Street. Thomas Augustin O'Shaughnessy, 1921. Width, 6 feet.*

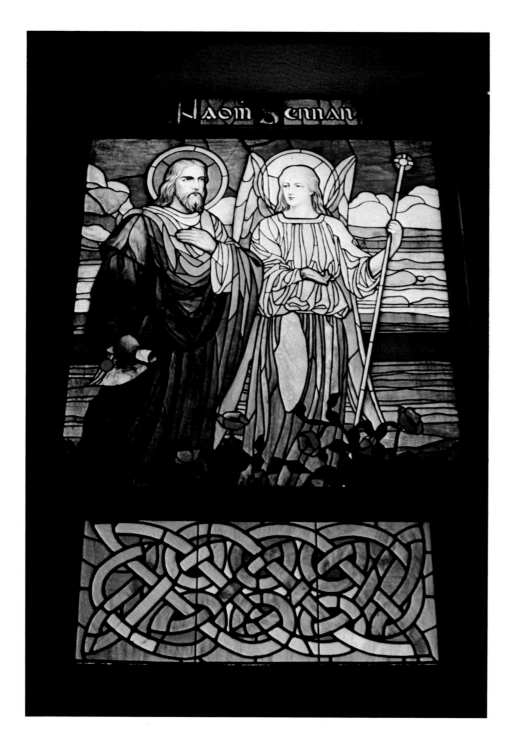

Left:

St. Sennan *window. St. Patrick's Church, 718 West Adams Street. Thomas Augustin O'Shaughnessy, 1912. Width, 4 feet.*

Right:

St. Carthage and St. Comgall. *St. Patrick Church, 718 West Adams Street, Thomas A. O'Shaughnessy, 1912. Width, 3 feet.*

DONATED BY MRS ELLEN COOGAN
IN MEMORY OF HER HUSBAND

John J. Kinsella Company

St. John Berchmans Church (1906-07) was erected for a Belgian congregation. Its windows of gorgeous coloration installed in 1921 show the masterful use of opalescent glass by the John J. Kinsella Company, specialists in ecclesiastical stained glass art. The broadly arched transept windows are huge, approximately 12 by 30 feet, and portray with power and imagination *The Blessed Sacrament* and *The Deluge,* the latter window dedicated to John J. Kinsella, the founder of the glass company. Smaller nave windows, together with such traditional subjects as *The Ascension* and *Christ Blessing the Children,* include a portrayal of St. Patrick and a dual study of Joan of Arc picturing her at the left as a simple peasant maid gazing heavenward for guidance, and at the right as a redoubtable military leader arrayed in steely blue armor.

St. James Lutheran Church (1916-17) has magnificent Kinsella windows of the Nativity, the Resurrection, and Gethsemane set in modified Gothic traceries and ornate perpendicular Gothic canopies. All are of exceptional technical and artistic merit, but the most outstanding for its balance of subject and color is the Gethsemane window. Especially moving is the kneeling figure of Christ seeking divine guidance, symbolized by the brilliant ray of light which shines down upon him.

Impressed by the Kinsella windows at St. James Lutheran Church, Archbishop George Mundelein in 1918 requested the company to create stained glass windows for the St. James Chapel of Quigley Preparatory Seminary North. The chapel is modeled after Sainte Chapelle in Paris in the French flamboyant Gothic style. Like Sainte Chapelle, it has tall narrow lancets filled with hundreds of medallions depicting religious scenes arranged in a sequence often found in medieval churches and cathedrals.

Eight triple lancets, each 10 feet wide and 40 feet high, on either side of the nave, picture in over two hundred medallions stories of the Old Testament and early Christian persons and events. Six double lancets in the chancel, each 7 by 30 feet, are devoted to the life, miracles, and parables of Christ. The west wall features a stunning rose window, twenty-eight feet in diameter, at the center of which stands the Virgin Mary encircled by sixteen radiating ruby red petals set with symbols of her many attributes.

The windows were designed by Robert Giles, an artist for the Kinsella Company. They are composed of thousands of small pieces of English antique glass in vibrant red, green, blue, and yellow with splashes of lavender and brown. Blackish brown oxide sparingly applied by the artist's wife delineates the facial features and other fine details. The St. James Chapel windows demonstrate the painstaking labor involved in assembling stained glass windows. It took over 150,000 pieces of glass to complete the chancel windows and over 500,000 for those in the nave.

The Deluge. *St. John Berchmans Church, 2517 West Logan Boulevard. John J. Kinsella Co., 1921. Width, 11 feet.*

TO THE GLORY OF GOD   AND IN MEMORY OF   JOHN J. KINSELLA

Left:

Gethsemane *window, east facade. St. James Evangelical Lutheran Church, 2048 North Fremont Street. John J. Kinsella Co., 1917. Width, approx., 10 feet.*

Right:

Rose window, west facade. St. James Chapel, Quigley Preparatory Seminary, North, 103 East Chestnut Street. Designed by Robert Giles of the John J. Kinsella Co., 1919. Width, 28 feet.

Giannini & Hilgart

Unique among the world's Christian churches is the Chicago Temple, the home of the First United Methodist Church, an eighteen-story skyscraper with a Gothic spire soaring 568 feet above street level. Erected in 1922-24, the building houses the Temple and space for commercial rentals, and is the fifth church to be built on the same site since 1838, the others having been destroyed by fire or rebuilt to accommodate the growing congregation.

Giannini & Hilgart installed the windows of traditional religious subjects for the church's sanctuary in the 1940s, and in 1965 the ten backlit windows at eye level in the small court of the building's east facade. The latter windows are of special interest to students of Chicago history because they picture the story of the Temple and its interaction with the growth of the city.

The scenes are framed in wide borders of scintillating red and blue antique glass. They picture, among others, the Rev. Jesse Walker, a pioneer Methodist circuit rider arriving at Fort Dearborn in 1825; the first church, a log cabin built in 1839; the second church, a classical Greek frame structure built in 1845; the third church, an imposing Second Empire edifice being consumed by the flames of the Great Fire; and a spectacular night scene featuring the building's great spire rising over the twinkling lights of the city.

Spire of First United Methodist Church. East facade, Chicago Temple, 77 West Washington Street. Giannini & Hilgart, 1965. Width, 2½ feet.

With the exception of the last one, all the studies were inspired by old Chicago prints and photographs. The windows were designed by Lubomyr Wandzura, a Chicago artist and a graduate of the School of the Art Institute. Wandzura had been the company's chief designer for many years before assuming its presidency in 1970, when he succeeded Fred Hilgart, the son of Fritz Hilgart, the founder of the firm.

In contrast to Giannini & Hilgart's smaller studies at the Chicago Temple is the firm's huge window in the contemporary style filling the entire north wall of St. Luke's Evangelical Lutheran Church. This modern-styled building was constructed in 1960 to replace the original church built in 1884 for a large German congregation. A non-figural composition, the window consists of great sweeping arcs of color symbolizing Christ "as the Light of the World" and "the Son of Righteousness rising with healing in His wings." The arcs from which the rays of color spring start at the bottom of the window with pale yellow, pale orange, and blue, then shift to rich red, dark blue, and finally into the blue of infinity. The window is composed entirely of French antique glass and is breathtaking in its radiance.

Left:

Chancel windows. St. Luke Evangelical Lutheran Church, 1500 West Belmont Avenue. Giannini & Hilgart, 1960. Each panel 10 feet wide and approx. 65 feet high.

Right:

Rose window, west facade. St. Sabina Church, 1210 West 78th Place. Giannini & Hilgart, 1933. Width, 21 feet.

Drehobl Bros. Art Glass Company

The Drehobl Bros. Art Glass Co. is now headed by Frank J. Drehobl, Jr., whose father and uncle founded the firm in 1919. Like Giannini & Hilgart, Drehobl has numerous ecclesiastical windows throughout the city. Among its finest, and showing the scope of the company's work, are those at Anshe Emet Synagogue. The seven windows in the auditorium installed between 1933 and 1934 were designed by Chicago artists Todros Geller and A. Raymond Katz, who created brilliantly colored, powerful studies expressive of Jewish life from ancient to modern times.

Almost fifty years later in 1981, the synagogue again called upon Drehobl to execute the *Twelve Tribes of Israel* windows for the Hall of Memories adjoining the auditorium. These windows were designed by Archie Rand, a New York City painter, muralist, and Hebrew scholar, who came to Chicago to work on the project with Drehobl and his master painter Thomas Snyder. The three men probably used the greatest variety of glasses employed by local glassmen on a single project. Incorporated into the windows are cathedral glass, bits of French and German antique glass, and even pieces of O'Shaughnessy's pot metal glass, which Drehobl says he uses only for special occasions. Although each window is a dynamic work of art in itself, all twelve should be considered as a unit to sense the full impact of their imagination and power.

A year later Rand again came to Chicago to collaborate with Drehobl and Snyder to produce the patriarch windows of Abraham, Isaac, and Jacob at Temple Sholom. Of these windows Rand explains: "It is the allover attention to detail, drawn from the respect I have and the care with which I approach tradition which finally unifies these compositions. I find that this evocative, rather than illustrative tack gives me avenues that are not as worn and provide the viewer with more stimulating fare."[8]

Twelve Tribes of Israel *windows. Hall of Memories, Anshe Emet Synagogue, 3760 North Pine Grove Avenue. Designed by Archie Rand, executed by Drehobl Bros. Art Glass Co., 1981. Each of twelve windows 63 inches wide.*

Left:

Detail, Isaac *window. Temple Sholom, 3480 North Lake Shore Drive. Designed by Archie Rand, executed by Drehobl Bros. Art Glass Co., 1982. Width, 2 feet.*

Right:

Detail, Our Lady of Czestochowa. *Immaculate Heart of Mary Church, 3834 North Spaulding Avenue. Drehobl Bros. Art Glass Co., 1970. Width, 2 feet.*

81

Years of Decline and the Art of Edgar Miller

Giannini & Hilgart and the Drehobl Bros. Art Glass Co. were among the few firms that managed to survive the Great Depression and World War II. Indeed, Frank Drehobl recalls his father saying that had it not been for the large Anshe Emet contract the company could not have stayed in business.

About the only important figure active in glass in Chicago during these years of decline was Edgar Miller, a versatile designer and craftsman who worked in stone and wood as well as in stained glass. Miller was born in Idaho in 1901 and came to Chicago in 1917 to study at the Art Institute. In 1925 his small panel of birds in vivid orange, blue, red, and yellow stained and painted glass won the Frank G. Logan Purchase Prize at the Art Institute.

In the early 1930s Miller and painter Sol Kogan began to restore and rehabilitate Victorian houses on West Burton Place and North Wells Street in what is now Old Town into attractive modern apartments. Miller often enhanced these properties with vibrantly colored small panels of fanciful animals, fish, and birds, or bold geometric compositions in which a stylized human figure occasionally appeared. Miller's original approach to glass attracted the attention of Earl H. Reed, Jr., a well-known Chicago architect, who wrote: "Few or no sketches are made ... the composition emerges full-blown, with superb finish, from the material itself. It is common for Miller to proceed boldly in lead and glass ... without benefit of cartoon, matching colors and cutting forms in accordance with a vivid and compelling inner sight."[9]

Miller's ability to work in a variety of styles is apparent in a pair of Art Deco panels, now owned by the Art Institute, which he designed for the Diana Court in the Michigan Square Building, a sophisticated Art Deco structure built by Holabird & Root in 1929, but since demolished. The style, which enjoyed a brief popularity in the 1920s, avoided stained glass for clear or tinted glass and highly polished brass, bronze, and chrome decorations of dazzling sunbursts, lightning bolts, flattened floral arrangements, and streamlined female figures. Miller's compositions of Diana, the Greek goddess of the hunt, are elegant examples of Art Deco and its use of clear plate glass sandblasted and etched.

Some glassmen had already gone out of business before the advent of Art Deco. Healy & Millet had dissolved their longtime partnership in 1899, while McCully & Miles, Schuler & Mueller, Mitchel & Halbach, and the Suess Ornamental Glass Company cannot be traced after 1920.

Diana the Huntress, *etched and sandblasted plate glass panels, formerly in Diana Court of the Michigan Square Building. The Art Institute of Chicago, Michigan Avenue at Adams Street. Edgar Miller, 1929. Width, 39½ inches.*

The economic slump of the 1930s also saw the demise of other major firms. Flanagan & Biedenweg, under different management, was no longer an important factor in the trade after 1930. The Kinsella Company was liquidated in 1931. The Temple Glass Company closed in 1933. In the same year Max Guler closed the Munich Studio and with several of his longtime associates went to work for the Drehobl brothers. To conserve his modest savings, O'Shaughnessy moved into his loft studio on West Superior Street in 1937, where he eked out a living painting church murals.

Despite the bleak economic picture, however, Chicago played host to the world at the Century of Progress Exposition of 1933, the last word in Art Deco and Art Moderne. Among the few buildings to have colored glass was the Hall of Religion which had windows by the Linden and Drehobl companies and by O'Shaughnessy. O'Shaughnessy also received a commission to design stained glass for twenty-three windows at the Illinois Host House. Among his presentations were such important Illinois historical events as Pere Marquette's explorations in Illinois, the Lincoln-Douglas debates, the opening of the Erie Canal, the World's Columbian Exposition of 1893, and a scene of the Century of Progress itself.

Interviewed by a reporter from the Chicago *Daily News* in 1937 about his work at the Host House, O'Shaughnessy declared that he had been promised $5000 but had never been paid a cent. The Host House award was probably the last large commission given to a single artist or studio during the Depression years. All the windows disappeared when the building was dismantled. As far as is known, not even a photograph remains.

The decline of stained glass art continued after World War II with the advent of the International style of architecture guided by Ludwig Mies van der Rohe and his disciples at the Illinois Institute of Technology. Precisely articulated in their steel frames and clear glass skins, Miesian structures, according to the style's practitioners, are their own decoration and need no other. Even Mies's St. Saviour Chapel on the IIT campus, as well as a number of the city's churches in his "bare-bones" style, make no concession to the art. Meanwhile in contrast, European architects and designers of religious as well as secular buildings have found new ways of using glass as a provocative and powerful means of expression.

Adolfas Valeska's Faceted Glass

Showing the influence of contemporary glassmen in France and Germany, but in a style all his own, has been the work of Adolfas Valeska, a painter, muralist, and decorator who specializes in stained glass using traditional and modern methods. Born in Kaunas, Lithuania, in 1901, Valeska graduated from the Kaunas School of Art and went on to study and work in Paris and Berlin.

Valeska immigrated to the United States in the late 1940s. After odd-jobbing in New York studios, he decided to move to Chicago, one of the reasons being that he had friends in Chicago's large Lithuanian community. In 1950 he opened the Valeska Art Studio, a three-storied workshop on North State Street, where he worked singlehandedly on his monumental windows, principally in slab glass and epoxy resin, which he favors over antique glass and leading because, he says, "they give me greater freedom of expression."

Typical of Valeska's large-scaled, tightly designed slab glass compositions are the two of Judaic studies at Rodfei Zedek Temple which won the Honor Award of the American Institute of Architects in 1966. In one window, "God, the Torah, and Israel are One" is inscribed in English. Its companion window carries the same message in ancient Aramaic. The lettering is subtly interwoven with age-old Judaic symbols of the menorah, the star of David, the shofar, the bowl of grapes, the oil lamp, the shin, the citron, and the palm branch. The windows are made entirely of small pieces of chipped and faceted slab glass which catch and reflect every nuance of the dazzling colors.

Chapel windows. Rodfei Zedek Temple, 5200 South Hyde Park Boulevard, Valeska Art Studio, 1968. Width, approx. 8 feet each.

In addition to other diverse works in the city, such as the large, symbol-laden windows on the themes of the Resurrection and Christian doctrine at the Cenacle Retreat House and the exuberant abstract designs at the 42nd Parallel Room at O'Hare International Airport, Valeska has charming examples of his work in his studio. One, the *Sacred Fish of Hawaii,* the result of a trip to the island, shows the movement of water and colorful fist swimming in its current. Another, in memory of a trip to Spain, depicts a farmer sowing seeds in the spring rain while an angel guiding a plow hovers over him. Still another window entitled *Exhibition Piece* is purely abstract and ornamental. All display Valeska's masterful command of color and technique in the new materials.

Bob White's Fused Glass

The only glassman to work in fused glass, the most difficult technique to master, and a field into which few have ventured, has been Bob White, a painter born in Oskaloosa, Iowa, in 1907. Retired in 1982, White has had a long and varied artistic career.

White's infatuation with stained glass began while he was studying painting in Europe. There he saw the great stained glass windows at Chartres Cathedral and, like many painters before him, was inspired to make stained glass his artistic medium. Upon his return to the United States in 1926, he procured a job with the Wilkes-Barre Art Glass Company and learned the basics of the craft by making "picture-postcard windows of stained glass saints."

In 1928 White left for New York City where he supported himself by doing "modern Gothic church windows." At the time the Whitney Studio Gallery, now the Whitney Museum, was looking for new works by American artists for its growing collection of modern American art. With nothing to lose, White took samples of his work to the director and to his amazement and delight was given a "carte blanche commission of $2000" to produce a window in his abstract style. That window led to a 1930 Guggenheim fellowship which he used for a return visit to Europe to make an intensive study of medieval stained glass techniques and designs.

Chapel window, south facade, Cenacle Retreat House, 513 West Fullerton Parkway. Valeska Art Stufio, 1967. Width, 22 feet.

When White came back to the United States, the Depression was in full swing. He was asked by Grant Wood, then supervisor of art in Iowa, to design stained glass, but with no funds forthcoming he left for Chicago where he was chosen director of a painting project for the Works Progress Administration. Later, after World War II, White taught painting on the West Coast. In 1954 he decided to "stay with stained glass for good" and moved back to Chicago where he was employed as a designer by the Clinton Glass Company. When the company closed in the early 1960s to make way for the Dan Ryan Expressway, White bought a sizable portion of their glass stock, set up a small workshop on the near North Side, and began the experiments that over a long period of years and many trials and failures eventually developed into his own fused glass technique.

White's fusions are formed on a base of clear sheet glass on which he places shards, chunks, and pulverized particles of clear or colored glass separated by thin metal strips to shape and direct the design. Over this he places a thin sheet of clear glass. The whole is then fired in a kiln where the heat causes the glass to melt and flow into swirls and ribbons of color. When annealed the glass is about an inch thick and has a smooth, slightly undulating surface on which White draws his delicate abstract paintings, bonding them permanently to the glass by another firing.

White's first full fusion in 1964 was a three-panel abstract study of Christ, now in a private Chicago collection, which won him a grant from the Louis Comfort Tiffany Foundation. In 1965 Chicago architect Ron Dirsmith commissioned White to design windows for a house he was remodeling on Burton Place. The following year the same architect commissioned him to create windows for the North Shore Unitarian Church in Deerfield, Illinois. For this project White designed twenty-three jewel-like panels set in a curving wall of rough white plaster.

These windows are arranged in three groups, conceived by the artist as a symphony in three movements. The first, the major grouping, deals with man's search for truth through science, mythology, and architecture and is visualized by such partial images as a sphinx, a plumed serpent, a Greek temple, Roman columns, a cathedral, and a spaceship. The second group focuses on such natural marvels as a rainbow, a rain forest, fossils, and a snowflake. The third suggests paths as yet unexplored by man on earth and beyond it into the outer reaches of space and the spectrum of light itself.

The only other fusion, made in 1974, that can be publicly viewed in the Chicago area is at Holy Name of Mary Church in the city. Entitled *Ecce Homo,* it is an intense, highly personal conception of Christ just before his crucifixion. One needs only to look upon Christ's anguished countenance, the awkward tilt of his head, his sagging body, and swollen hands bound in cords to understand how deeply the artist felt Christ's agony.

White's largest commmission (1972) was for the First Presbyterian Church in Mason City, Iowa. It consists of 215 fusions, each 25 feet high, on the theme of the Creation as found in Genesis, but interpreted in contemporary scientific terms to express "the creative forces for our existence as we know it today."

New Directions

Since the revival of stained glass in the 1960s, a number of new studios and workshops have been springing up in Chicago and its environs. At midyear 1982 there were fifteen in the city and twenty-one in the suburbs. Some of their designers, like those on the West Coast, are producing highly original autonomous panels for homes and offices. But there is no great demand for their work. In the main, the majority of these artists and craftsmen depend for their livelihood on small domestic commissions and repairs and on the sale of glass, tools, and materials needed for the workshops they conduct for the growing number of stained glass enthusiasts.

What is really needed for a revival of the art in Chicago is a renewed understanding of stained glass as an ornamental and structural material by local architects. The 1 South Wacker Building designed by Helmut Jahn (1982-83), completely sheathed in silver, coral, and black glass suggests what might be a new direction. Or perhaps it is a fulfillment of what Frank Lloyd Wright had envisioned when he wrote:

"Imagine a city iridescent by day, luminous by night . . . Buildings, shimmering fabrics, woven of rich glass; glass all clear or part opaque and part clear, patterned in color or stamped to harmonize with the metal tracery that is to hold all together, the metal tracery to be, in itself, a thing of delicate beauty consistent with slender steel construction, expressing the nature of that construction in the mathematics of structure . . . I dream of such a city."[10]

One South Wacker Building. Designed by Helmut Jahn of Murphy/Jahn, architects, 1982.

90

Art Glass from Elsewhere 3

Madonna in glory. *Center panels of five-lancet, east balcony window. St. Gertrude Church, 1420 West Granville Avenue. Franz Mayer & Co., Munich, Germany, 1931. Width of each panel approx. 3 feet.*

Chapter Three

Of the thousands of stained glass windows installed in Chicago during the city's stained glass heyday, about seventy-five per cent were made by local glassmen and the balance by designers and studios from the eastern states and Europe. Prominent among the Americans were: Louis Comfort Tiffany, John LaFarge, and Edward Peck Sperry of New York City; Charles J. Connick of Boston; and the Willett Studios of Philadelphia. European firms supplying glass to Chicago were principally German and of these the Franz Mayer Company and F. X. Zettler, Royal Bavarian Art Institute, both of Munich, Germany, were the largest competitors for the local business.

After the Depression and World War II, Chicago's decline as an important art glass center left the field wide open for outsiders. At the present time the Drehobl Company, Giannini & Hilgart, and Botti Studio of Architectural Arts all do a thriving local and nationwide business. But they must compete here and elsewhere with Connick and Willett; Emil Frei Associates of St. Louis; the Conrad Schmitt Studios of New Berlin, Wisconsin; and the Conrad Pickel Studio of Vero Beach, Florida. The world-acclaimed Gabriel Loire Studio of Chartres has also been a formidable competitor.

All these studios have made important contributions to Chicago's vast collection of ecclesiastical and secular stained glass art. Enriching it still more have been outstanding works by the eminent English collaborators Sir Edward Burne-Jones and William Morris; the distinguished American painter Abraham Rattner in conjunction with the Barillet Studio of Paris; and the world-renowned Russian painter Marc Chagall in partnership with Charles Marq of the Atelier Jacques Simon of Reims, France.

Edward Burne-Jones and William Morris

Chicago is fortunate to have two windows of exquisite design by Burne-Jones and William Morris, the now legendary partners who played key roles in the stained glass revival of the nineteenth century. These windows are of inestimable value, for only a handful of works by these artists exist in the United States.

The windows picture *St. Margaret* and *St. Cecilia* and are located in the vestibule on either side of the main entrance of the Second Presbyterian Church. St. Margaret is to the left and St. Cecilia to the right as one faces the windows. St. Margaret, robed in rich red, is entwined by her proverbial dark green dragon, upon whose body she nonchalantly rests a daintily sandaled foot. St. Cecilia, the patron saint of music, is draped in velvety purple and blue and dreamily plays a portable organ in a lush green forest. Both are typical Burne-Jones figures, ethereal and willowy. As in hundreds of other windows made in collaboration with Burne-Jones (who drew only the figurative cartoons), Morris chose the colors of the glasses, composed the bold lead lines, and painted the hands, faces, drapery folds, and delicate grisaille work.

St. Margaret *and* St. Cecilia. *Vestibule, Second Prestyterian Church, 1936 South Michigan Avenue. Designed by Edward Burne-Jones, executed by William Morris, c. 1900. Width, 2 feet each.*

sancta margarita

To the glory of God
and in memory of
Franklin Darius Gray
Born May 19 1818 Died November 19 1905

sancta cecilia

To the glory of God
and in memory of
Ann Olive Phelps Gray
Born May 24 1822 Died July 7 1899

These treasures are replicas of two windows designed by Burne-Jones for Christ Church Cathedral, Oxford, and were purchased and brought to Chicago by Franklin Darius Gray, founder of Chicago's National Safe Deposit Company. Gray was also on the Board of Directors of the First National Bank and a member of the Second Presbyterian Church. Gray may have seen the windows at Christ Church and there is some conjecture that he had commissioned replicas directly from William Morris before the latter's death in 1896. The windows were displayed for the first time in Chicago around 1902 by Joseph Twyman, an Englishman and Morris disciple, in the William Morris Memorial Room at the Tobey Furniture Company, of which Twyman was the chief designer. At what point Gray gave the windows to the church is not known, but an article appearing in *House Beautiful* in December, 1904 establishes that he had done so by that date. They were dedicated to Gray and his wife, Ann Olive Phelps Gray, in 1906.

La Farge and Tiffany

A comparison of the careers of John La Farge (1835-1910) and Louis Comfort Tiffany (1848-1933) reveals that these foremost artists in American stained glass had much in common. Both were natives of New York City, both began as painters, and both were pioneers in the discovery and development of opalescent glass.

La Farge first studied painting with Thomas Couture in Paris and later with William Morris Hunt of Newport, Rhode Island. Tiffany was a pupil of George Inness, the great American landscape painter, and later studied with Leon Bailly in Paris. Tiffany won considerable acclaim as a genre and landscape painter, while La Farge, the superior painter, achieved fame as a muralist and a painter of landscapes, still lifes, and figures.

Influenced by the English Arts and Crafts Movement and by William Morris, both Americans turned to the decorative arts and interior decoration where they discovered that stained glass, as opposed to painting, offered them a larger scope for their artistic expression. Both men, working independently, began to experiment with combinations of metallic oxides at the Heidt glasshouse in Brooklyn about 1876. Their purpose, in addition to developing richer colors and a wider range of textures, was to dispense with paint and to allow, for the first time, the glass itself to define light, shading, and perspective. From this point on their approaches were entirely different.

As Robert Koch has pointed out: "La Farge's aim was to use glass in windows as a painter's medium," while Tiffany's was "to exploit the properties of the glass itself in the decoration of interiors." Aside from this, however, as Koch goes on, "both made their first ornamental windows of opalescent glass in 1876; both installed their first windows in 1878; and both worked for the same architect on the same job in 1880."[1] Moreover, both were granted patents for opalescent glass in 1880, La Farge for his version in February and Tiffany in November of the same year.

Detail of Tiffany window on page 102.

At first the two had exchanged ideas and discoveries on friendly terms. In fact, Tiffany even offered La Farge a partnership in his rapidly expanding business. When Tiffany unabashedly reneged on his offer, the men became bitter rivals and fierce competitors. Unable to compete with Tiffany's inborn flair for showmanship and unlimited capital (Tiffany was heir to the family fortune of Tiffany & Company founded by his jeweler father), La Farge gradually assumed a lesser position, while Tiffany went on to ever greater public acclaim.

Tiffany was at the height of his popularity from 1880 to about 1910. By 1920 his style was dated and his work relegated to attics or sold to secondhand dealers. In recent years, however, the renewed interest in his art has literally brought Tiffany glass out of the closet into the marketplace where a favrile vase, lamp, or art glass window now sells for thousands of dollars. More to the point is that Tiffany's work is once again being recognized for its artistry and beauty and not only for its monetary value.

La Farge Glass in Chicago

John La Farge has only one window in Chicago, *The Angel in the Lilies* at the Second Presbyterian Church, which also houses a fine collection of Tiffany stained glass. This window is said to have been purchased by the congregation at the World's Columbian Exposition of 1893. Although the church is cautious about attributing the work to La Farge, the Pre-Raphaelite style, the exceptionally heavy glass laminations, and the striking resemblance of the angel's features to those of figures in other windows by him, all lead to the conclusion that the work is indeed authentic.

The influence of the Pre-Raphaelites, whom La Farge personally knew, is seen in the trance-like posture of the winged angel, her ecstatic expression, and the massed field of lilies in which she stands. The long folds of the angel's grayish brown robe and the chunks of milk white opalescent glass which shape the lilies are unusually thick, varying from one to four inches.

The Second Presbyterian Church also had a great rose window by La Farge which was destroyed in the church fire of 1900 and was replaced by Tiffany's *The Ascension* and *The Five Scourges* in 1918.

Tiffany Glass in Chicago

The fourteen windows by Louis C. Tiffany at the Second Presbyterian Church offer visitors a rare opportunity to examine at close range the various techniques he invented to eliminate the use of paint except for facial features, hair, hands, and feet. As Tiffany explained: "By the aid of studies in chemistry and through years of experiments, I have found means to avoid the use of paint, etching or burning, or otherwise treating the surface of the glass so that it now becomes possible to produce figures in glass of which even the flesh tones are not superficially treated—built up of what I call "genuine glass."[2]

The earliest Tiffany window in the church, about 1890, is *The Peace Window,* an elaborate mosaic in the twelfth and thirteenth century medallion style. Three gracefully interwoven medallions carry angels, the center one unrolling a scroll inscribed with the word PEACE. Flat pieces of antique glass in blue, green, red, and gold give the window its soft diffused glow.

Tiffany's *Christ Blessing the Little Children* was originally installed in the First Presbyterian Church in 1893 and removed to its present location in 1913. The subject, used many times by Tiffany as well as by other stained glass artists of his time, is based on a popular religious painting by Bernhard Plonkhurst.

Attention centers on the seated, haloed figure of Christ holding a contented infant in his lap. The other children, one bearing a gift of fruit in a small bowl, look at him with adoration. Through the open door of the hut one catches a glimpse of clear blue sky and clusters of vines that sway in a barely perceptible breeze. Although the scene is resplendent in rich amber and red, it conveys its message with simplicity.

The Jeweled Window (1895), another mosaic, focuses upon a small center panel containing a faceted gold Greek cross set against a background of green leaves and rosettes. Below the cross is an amphora in burnt sienna bearing the initials IHS, the first three Greek letters in the name Jesus. Two rich borders of opalescent glass in the dominant colors of gold and burnt sienna frame and emphasize the inner study.

A notable example of Tiffany's secular work in a religious setting is *The Pastoral Window,* dating from about 1918, the only signed Tiffany window in the church. In this study the Creator and nature are one. A profusion of purple iris in the foreground borders a running stream that leads to verdant forests and distant hazy blue mountains surmounted by a pearly pink sky. All the colors and shading come from within the opalescent glass itself. No paint was used.

Detail, Angel in the Lilies. *Second Presbyterian Church, 1936 South Michigan Avenue. John La Farge, New York, 1893. Full width of window, 9 feet.*

Left:

Peace Window. *Second Presbyterian Church, 1936 South Michigan Avenue. Tiffany Studios, New York, 1890. Width, 9 feet.*

Right:

Detail, Christ Blessing the Little Children. *Second Presbyterian Church. Tiffany Studios, New York, 1893. Full width, 9 feet.*

Left:

Jeweled Window. *Second Presbyterian Church. Tiffany Studios, 1895. Width, 9 feet.*

Right:

Pastoral Window. *Second Presbyterian Church, 1936 South Michigan Avenue. Tiffany Studios, New York, c. 1918. Width, 9 feet.*

Centered high in the balcony of the east facade is *The Ascension* and immediately below it *The Five Scourges,* all installed between 1918-19. In *The Ascension* gold and silver dust sprayed onto the glass before it cooled produced the iridescence for which Tiffany is famous. The folds of Christ's white robe and those of the hosts of winged angels encircling him are formed of Tiffany drapery glass.

In the striking studies of *The Five Scourges,* prism-shaped pieces of glass in brilliant red, blue, and green set at sharp angles catch the constantly changing rays of light that flash about the grim visages of the figures bearing the whip, the crown of thorns, the cross, the hammer and the nails, and the rope. Air bubbles and other flaws in the glass intensify the coruscating colors.

Tiffany's remaining windows, all of opalescent glass in mauve, soft green, gray, and blue depict such traditional scenes as: *The Angel at the Open Tomb, The Mount of the Holy Cross, St. Paul Preaching to the Athenians,* and *Behold the Lamb of God.*

Other churches in Chicago that also possess Tiffany windows are the Church of Our Saviour which has five and Hyde Park Union Church which has four. The latter houses an especially fine study of *St. Paul at Mars Hill,* notable for its marvelous iridescence.

Of Tiffany's secular works in the city, three are superb mosaics. Two were designed by J.A. Holzer, a staff artist for the Tiffany Studio. These are: the intricate designs of colored stone, mother-of-pearl, and favrile glass set in marble in the lobby, stairwell, and mezzanine on the Washington Street side of the Chicago Public Library Cultural Center; and the 120-ft. frieze in the rotunda of the Marquette Building depicting the exploration of the Northwest Passage by Marquette and Joliet in 1673. The third is the great triple-domed ceiling constructed of 2,500,000 pieces of shimmering blue favrile glass on the Washington Street side of the Marshall Field State Street Store.

The Tiffany Studio was also responsible for two imposing skylight domes at the Cultural Center—one over Preston Bradley Hall, the other in the lobby leading to the G.A.R. room at the north end of the building.

There are also numerous signed Tiffany windows in the Rosehill Cemetery Mausoleum. One of the most striking of these is the John G. Shedd Memorial triptych, *The Angel of Truth,* installed in 1912. Reinforced only by plated sections of glass, this window caused considerable controversy in its day because of its absence of leadlines and crossbars. Finally, tucked away in the H.N. Higginbotham Hall of the Field Museum of Natural History is a delightful Tiffany Art Nouveau window of a mermaid frolicking with a golden-scaled fish, in which the swirling movement of the water is simulated by rippled cathedral glass and air bubbles by smooth white cabochons.

Above right:

The Ascension. *Second Presbyterian Church, 1936 South Michigan Avenue. Tiffany Studios, New York, c. 1918. Width, 19 feet.*

Below:

Dome in Preston Bradley Hall. Chicago Public Library Cultural Center, 78 East Washington Street, Tiffany Studios, 1897. Diameter, 40 feet.

Edward Peck Sperry

Like J.A. Holzer, Frederick Wilson, and others, Edward Peck Sperry was one of Tiffany's most accomplished staff artists. Like them, he frequently worked independently of the Tiffany Studio and was also artist-in-chief for the Church Glass & Decorating Company of New York City. Sperry specialized in making large-scale pictorial windows, of which Chicago has two impressive examples—the *Success Window* and the *Ivanhoe Window,* both memorial windows executed by the Church company.

The *Success Window* was donated by the employees of the meat packing firm of Armour & Company and commemorates Philip Danforth Armour, Jr., the son of the founder, who died at the age of thirty-one in 1900. The window was installed the same year in the stairwell of the main building of Armour Institute (now the Illinois Institute of Technology).

A dignified work conceived in the classical Greek style, the window consists of three large panels of opalescent glass enclosed in an entablature of Carrara marble. The central panel, symbolizing Success, depicts a vigorous young man accepting the crown of Triumph from the altar of Fame. Each of the two outer panels shows two female figures representing Heat, Light, Gravity, and Motion, elements of nature suggestive of the scientific subjects taught at the Institute.

Center panel of Success *triptych. Armour Institute Main Building, now Illinois Institute of Technology, 10 West 33rd Street. Edward Peck Sperry, New York, 1903. Width of center panel, 4 feet.*

FAMAM
FACTIS
EXTENDIT

IN · MEMORY · OF
PHILIP · D · ARMOUR · Jr

Larger in scale and more dramatic in concept than the *Success Window* is Sperry's *Ivanhoe Window* installed in 1903 in the east facade above the main entryway of the Frank Dickinson Bartlett Memorial Gymnasium on the University of Chicago campus. The window commemorates Frank Dickinson Bartlett who died at the age of twenty. Young Bartlett was the son of Adolphus Clay Bartlett, a trustee of the university and a partner in the huge wholesale hardware firm of Hibbard, Spencer, Bartlett & Company. Bartlett funded the construction of the gymnasium and William G. Hibbard, also a partner in the hardware firm, donated the window.

Constructed of over 15,000 pieces of opalescent and rippled glass, the window depicts the famous scene from Sir Walter Scott's *Ivanhoe* in which the victorious knight, having won all of the second day's battles at the great tournament held outside the ramparts of Ashby de la Zouche, is about to receive his award from the Lady Rowena. To the right of the window, the blond bareheaded knight, a white silken tunic flung over his shining armor, kneels before the Saxon princess who descends from her throne in a flowing white robe to bestow the crown upon the champion. To the left is the imperious Prince John mounted on a magnificently caparisoned steed and accompanied by his formidable retinue arrayed in steely blue armor. Lending additional color and animation to the dramatic scene are the richly attired lords and ladies who cheer the hero of the day from the tiered stands on either side of the battlefield.

Joining in the festivities are townsfolk, squires, and pages who carry standards, streamers, and pennants emblazoned with coats of arms in brilliant red, blue, green, purple, and gold. These draw the eye upward to the window's dark oak traceries through which appear the tall verdant trees around the jousting arena. In the distance, above the leafy treetops, in dappled shades of green and blue, can be seen the tranquil walled and turreted town of Ashby.

Surmounting the splendid scene is a gold perpendicular Gothic canopy, and higher still gold medallions set with glowing amethysts, magnificent decorations in keeping with the window's Gothic spirit and the Neo-Gothic building which houses it.

Ivanhoe Window. *Bartlett Memorial Gymnasium, 5640 South University Avenue. Edward Peck Sperry, New York, 1903. Width, 19 feet.*

Mayer and Zettler Munich Windows

About the same time that Sperry was working on the Armour and Bartlett memorials, "Munich-styled" windows began to appear in large numbers in Chicago churches. Most of these windows were made by the Franz Mayer Company and F. X. Zettler, Royal Bavarian Art Institute of Munich, Germany, both of which opened branch offices in Chicago in the early 1900s. They met with instant success, partly because of the local glassmen's strike and also because they had a sensitive understanding of the religious subject matter desired by the Bohemian, German, and Polish congregations who were then building churches in the city's ethnic neighborhoods.

Mayer and Zettler were hardly newcomers to the trade, for they were already well established in the 1840s and recognized in Europe and the United States for their fine craftsmanship. Except for a few works based on Italian Renaissance paintings, Mayer and Zettler windows are in the German Baroque style.

Munich windows have sometimes been disparaged for their sentimentality. Some, admittedly, are overly sweet, but no more so than many of Tiffany's productions. As James L. Sturm has pointed out, "much of the criticism of Munich glass stems from the simple prejudice against its style rather than the manner in which it was executed."[3]

St. Cecilia. *St. Michael's Church, 1633 North Cleveland Avenue. Franz Mayer & Co., Munich, Germany, 1903. Width, 6½ feet.*

Windows by the Franz Mayer Company appear in at least seven Chicago churches. Among the earliest (1902), are those at St. Michael's Redemptorist Church erected between 1866-69 for a German congregation. The immense round-arched windows in the nave are devoted to saints and prophets. Each is embellished with exceptionally wide borders filled with flowers and vines and exuberant canopies.

Another window, seldom noticed because of its location in the organ loft six stories above the ground floor, is a study of St. Cecilia, a favorite of middle-European congregants. Contemplative and serene, the patron saint of music is watched over by angels and cherubim as she performs on her legendary organ. The attention to decorative detail characteristic of the Munich style is seen in the patterned curtain and the elaborately carved organ and capitals supporting the vaulted arches.

The sixteen windows at St. Alphonsus Church erected between 1889-97, also for a German congregation, portray episodes in the lives of Christ, Mary, and St. Alphonsus. A typical panel, for instance, is *The Betrothal of Mary and Joseph,* which displays the customary curtain behind which appear triple arches with fancifully carved columns and behind these an elegantly rendered rib-vaulted ceiling framed in a wide border of realistic floral patterns.

Zettler windows appear in at least seventeen Chicago churches. About the earliest of their works are those signed and dated 1903 at St. Stanislaus Kostka Church (1881), the mother of all Polish churches in Chicago. The sixteen windows in the nave are devoted to the mysteries of the rosary. Each consists of a small center panel elaborately bordered with an inner frame containing marble columns and arches festooned with vines and garlands and a wide outer border of a lacy valentine-like pattern filled with twisting vines, doves of peace, angels, and bouquets of red and yellow roses.

As in many Munich windows, the leadlines normally integral to the design tend to fade into and become subordinate to the sometimes overly painted surface.

Among the most spectacular windows in the city, both in the Renaissance style, are Zettler's *Pentecost* and *Last Judgment* windows, each 21 by 62 feet, at St. Michael's Church, built in 1907 for a Polish Catholic congregation. In the *Pentecost* window, the prayerful Mary is seated on an elaborately carved throne. Gathered about her are the apostles in various postures of prayer. Above Mary are huge carved columns from which spring great arches and vaults. Above Mary's head is a burst of white and gold light symbolizing the presence of God. In the brilliant center of light is a dove representing the Holy Spirit. Surmounting the grand scene is an immense Gothic canopy in which angels posed on marble pedestals stand and kneel in prayerful attitudes.

Mayer and Zettler continued to have offices in Chicago until the Great Depression. The last traceable Mayer installations, dated 1939, are the windows in St. Bartholomew Church; the last by Zettler (1959-60) are in the Assumption Greek Orthodox Church.

Nativity, *lunette in vestibule. St. Boniface Church, 921 North Noble Street. F. X. Zettler, Royal Bavarian Art Institute, Munich, Germany, 1904. Width, 6½ feet. The church has since closed.*

Left:

Detail, Pentecost Window, east transept. St. Michael Church, 83rd Street and South Shore Drive. F. X. Zettler, Royal Bavarian Art Institute, Munich, Germany, 1909. Width, 21 feet.

Right:

Detail, Immaculate Conception Window, south facade. St. Thomas Aquinas Church, 5112 West Washington Boulevard. F. X. Zettler, Munich, 1925. Width of detail, 7 feet.

Willett Stained Glass Studios

The renowned Willett Stained Glass Studios of Philadelphia were founded by the master designer and glass painter William Willett (1867?-1921). Willett, born in New York City, studied painting with John La Fargo and probably developed his interest in stained glass from his association with the eminent New York artist and glassman. After an intensive study of stained glass in Europe, Willett returned to the United States and was employed as a designer for a Pittsburgh studio before establishing his own studio in Philadelphia in 1898.

Upon William Willett's death, his son Henry Lee Willett assumed the business and artistic direction of the firm. At the present time his son E. Crosby Willett is chairman of the board. The studio, now the largest in the United States, has installations throughout the country, as well as in Oslo, Norway, and Krakow, Poland. The Willett Studio has always been progressive in its outlook and was among the first in the United States to work with slab glass.

Christ in Glory. *Chapel, Church of the Atonement, 5749 North Kenmore Avenue. Willett Stained Glass Studio, Philadelphia, 1925. Width, 7 feet.*

In Chicago there are Willett installations in at least thirty-three buildings, both religious and secular. Among their many windows are two splendid studies of *Christ Enthroned*. One is in the north wall of a small Gothic-styled chapel at the Episcopal Church of the Atonement; the other fills the south wall above the altar in the Hilton Chapel of the Chicago Theological Seminary. Each is heavily painted on fine antique glass, but retains its jewel-like radiance because of the exceptionally delicate and sensitive brushwork.

There are also fine triple-lancet windows in the west wall of the Hilton Chapel containing frontal figures of saints, evangelists, and prophets painted on clear glass. Each figure, robed predominantly in brilliant red and blue, stands on a pedestal adorned with opaque white jewels set against an unusual background of opaque white oblongs. The skillful use of white thrusts the figures forward, giving them a life-like three-dimensional appearance.

The sensitivity and versatility of the Willett Studios may be seen in the windows of the Church of the Ascension. In 1925 the well-known Boston firm of Reynolds, Francis & Rohnstock had installed a three-part lancet window based on the theme of the rosary. Forty-one years later in 1966 the church called upon the Willett Studio to continue the same theme in the remaining four windows in the north wall of the church. Although the Willett style is freer than that of the Boston firm, it blends perfectly with the earlier format in scale and coloration. Surrounding the small figurative panels and reaching into the traceries is some of the finest grisaille painting to be seen in the city.

Of the several slab glass windows the studio has in Chicago, one of the largest (20 by 50 feet) and most powerful is the window installed in 1974 in the meditation chapel of St. Mary of Nazareth Hospital. Upon entering the chapel, the visitor is overwhelmed by the window's brilliant colors which completely dominate the small room.

A close study of the window reveals that it contains highly abstract symbolism on the theme of the Sacrament. In the center of the window is a huge red whorl which suggests a monstrance supported on a stem. The center of the monstrance is white, symbolizing God's presence. The upper left of the window shows a stalk of wheat and the upper right grapes, representing the bread and wine of the Sacrament.

page 119

Left:
Detail, chapel windows, theme of the Sacrament. St. Mary of Nazareth Hospital, 2233 West Division Street. Willett Stained Glass Studios, Philadelphia, 1974. Width, 20 feet.

Right:
Nave window. Hilton Chapel of chicago Theological Seminary, 5757 South University Avenue. Willett Stained Glass Studios, Philadelphia, 1926. Width, approx., 5½ feet.

Charles J. Connick Associates

The best known traditionalist among the American artists who sought to revive medieval stained glass styles and methods was Charles J. Connick (1875-1945). Connick began his career as a cartoonist with a Pittsburgh newspaper but gave up his job for an apprenticeship with a local stained glass studio. After studying stained glass in Europe, he returned to the United States in the early 1900s and went to Boston where he met architect Ralph Adams Cram, a passionate medievalist who designed churches in the Gothic style. Connick's windows and Cram's architecture were mutually compatible, as were the two men, and Cram commissioned Connick to design many of the windows for his churches. Cram also helped Connick to set up his studio in Boston in 1912.

Unlike William Willett, Henry Wynd Young, J. Gordon Guthrie, Ernest Lakeman, and others who sought to modify the medieval spirit of stained glass, Connick firmly believed that only a strict adherence to medieval methods could restore the medium to the transcendent position it had held in the twelfth and thirteenth centuries. The studio has never deviated from its policy of using the finest antique glass and has shunned opalescent glass because, as Connick maintained, its "milky or opalescent texture detracted from the clarity of the material."

After Connick died, his longtime associate Orin E. Skinner assumed the aesthetic direction of the company and continued to make windows in the Connick tradition. Connick windows can be found in religious and secular buildings throughout the country and in Chicago they appear in at least five churches.

One of the projects which Cram and Connick created together is Chicago's Fourth Presbyterian Church. In accord with the Gothic ideal, the sanctuary is high and narrow and dominated on the west facade by a great chancel arch which contains three large windows by Connick, the center one a study of the resurrected Christ. Six lancet windows in the east facade, for which Cram provided elaborate tracery, are filled with Connick portrayals of the apostles and evangelists. The principle color of all these windows is blue, which Connick used consistently in all his windows, partly out of "personal preference" and also because he adhered to Viollet-le-Duc's scientific analysis that blue was the active agent in medieval windows.

Of the forty-seven art glass windows at Hyde Park Union Church, one is by Zettler and four are by Tiffany. The rest are by Connick and were installed over a forty-year period from 1921 to 1961. The windows are devoted to the parables of Christ and to portrayals of various saints and prophets. There is also a splendid rose window by Connick in the east facade.

Close by Hyde Park Union Church is Bond Chapel, a Gothic gem nestled within the medieval setting of the University of Chicago campus, a perfect

East facade window. Fourth Presbyterian Church, 126 East Chestnut Street. Charles J. Connick Associates, Boston, 1928. Width, 16 feet.

120

location for Connick windows. This lovely chapel is filled with soft, shimmering light from the radiant windows on all four sides of the sanctuary; it gives one the feeling of being in a jewel box. The six windows on either side of the nave express the mysteries of the Christian faith and are banded along the bottom by quotations from the Scriptures. Although the imagery is impressive, it is surpassed by that in the window above the altar which displays a comprehensive spectacle of the whole of the New Testament beginning with the activities of Jesus and his disciples, the spread of the faith, and its culmination in the vision of the Apocalypse.

Blue still dominates the Connick palette in the beautiful *Such is the Kingdom of Heaven* window of 1950 at the First Presbyterian Church at Lake Forest, Illinois. But the much painted work is enlivened by the use of gold, deep rose, aqua, green, and purple. It is interesting in this church to compare the Connick window and one by Henry Wynd Young, both of antique glass, with those of opalescent glass by Tiffany.

Left:

Detail, east facade window. Bond Chapel. 1050 East 59th Street. Charles J. Connick Associates, Boston, 1926.

Right:

Such is the Kingdom of Heaven. *First Presbyterian Church, Lake Forest, Illinois. Connick Associates, 1955. Width, approx., 6 feet.*

Conrad Schmitt Studios

Unlike Connick Associates, the Conrad Schmitt Studios of New Berlin, Wisconsin, has worked with many glasses in many different styles. The studio was established in 1889 by Conrad Schmitt, a native of Milwaukee. Since its inception the studio has maintained a large decorating department and works in bronze, marble, iron, and wood, as well as in stained glass.

When Conrad Schmitt died, his sons Rupert and Edward continued the business. After their deaths, Bernard O. Gruenke, who had been associated with the studio since 1936, purchased the business and continued its operation under the name of the founder. Gruenke is a graduate of the Layton School of Art and was a student at the Corcoran Art School in Washington, D.C. Shortly after World War II Gruenke visited Europe and brought back with him from France a box of slab glass with which he assembled one of the first faceted glass panels in the United States. The window, entitled *Christ in Judgment,* is on display at the Schmitt studios.

Gruenke is still active as the firm's aesthetic director while his son Bernard E. Gruenke is president. The studio windows are installed "in all the states of the Union and in four foreign countries." As the younger Gruenke writes: "The studio has no one particular style and executes work of its own as well as that of other designers." In Chicago Schmitt windows appear in eleven ecclesiastical and secular buildings.

In the late 1940s the Schmitt Studio installed all the windows at St. Peter's Episcopal Church. These were designed in a modified Gothic style to harmonize with the Neo-Gothic architecture. The predominant color of the windows is a vivid blue, subdued by the use of much white and touches of gold, rose, lavender, and pale green.

The large central figure in the chancel window depicts the Transfiguration, Jesus standing with outstretched arms between Moses and Elias. Peter, James, and John are seen in a lower panel. The window over the vestibule shows Christ standing in a large medallion giving the keys of the kingdom of heaven to a kneeling St. Peter. Smaller medallions on either side of Christ portray the four evangelists. A series of small lights on either side of the nave and in the clerestory bear symbols from the Old and New Testaments.

Right:
Jesus gives Peter the Keys of the Kingdom. *St. Peter's Episcopal Church, 621 West Belmont Avenue. Conrad Schmitt Studios, New Berlin, Wisconsin, c. 1948. Width, 10 feet.*

Page 126:
The Glory of the Ascension, *north transept window. St. William Church, 2600 North Sayre Street. Conrad Schmitt Studios, New Berlin, Wisconsin, 1960. Width, 22 feet.*

Page 127:
Rose window, south facade. St. Vincent de Paul Church, 1010 West Webster Avenue. Conrad Schmitt Studios, New Berlin, Wisconsin, 1955. Width, 22 feet.

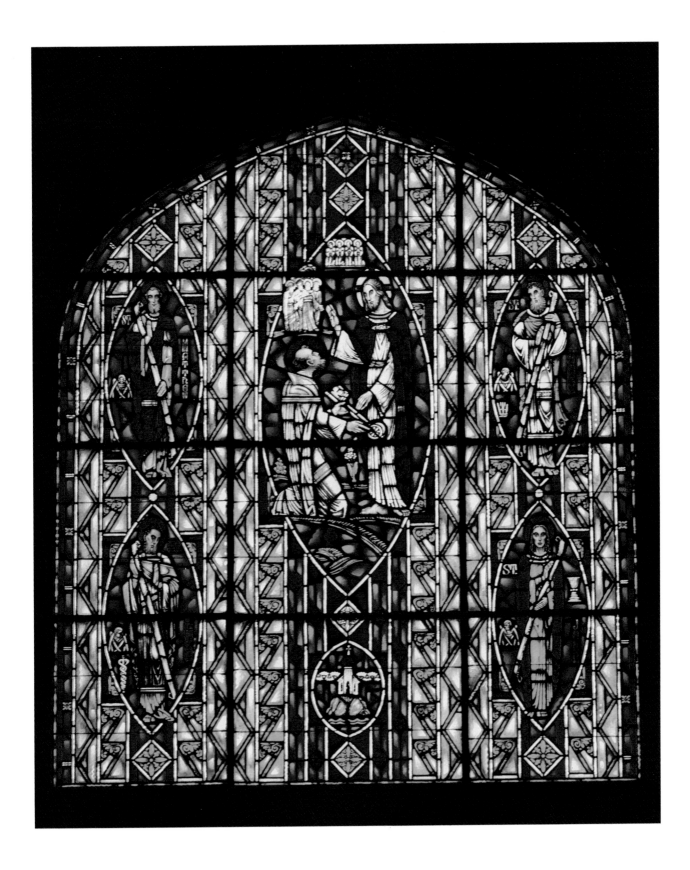

An outstanding work of the Schmitt Studios is the great rose window, twenty-two feet in diameter, installed in the south facade of St. Vincent de Paul Church. This window replaced a rose window of St. Cecilia by Thomas Augustin O'Shaughnessy which was destroyed by a fire in 1955. The rose is composed of thousands of small pieces of red, blue, gold, and orange antique glass, each separately leaded into a complex geometric design. Only the minutest details of the angels' faces and robes and the wings of the doves are painted. The window is a burst of glory, at the center of which is the Sun of Splendor, symbolizing God from whom all blessings radiate. Eight doves around the Sun represent the eight beatitudes while twelve angels, each holding a star, symbolize the twelve divine praises.

When the Schmitt Studio received the commission for the windows of the contemporary-styled St. William Church in 1957, it chose slab glass in more than forty-four brilliant colors for the semi-abstract composition of biblical figures and liturgical symbols. When the light strikes these pieces of faceted glass, they produce an infinite number of subtle tonalities which dapple the interior of the church with a magical aura of color.

Emil Frei Associates

Four generations of the Frei family have been producing stained glass windows in St. Louis since 1904. Emil Frei, Sr., a graduate of the School of Arts and Crafts in Munich, Germany was, like Conrad Schmitt, employed by the Franz Mayer Company before coming to the United States in the 1890s. After a short stay with a San Francisco decorating studio, he left for St. Louis to establish his own business.

When Emil Frei died in 1941, his son Emil, Jr. became president. The younger Frei was a graduate of the School of Fine Arts of Washington University in St. Louis. His son Robert Frei also attended the School of Fine Arts at Washington University and worked under the direction of his father until the latter's death in 1969. Robert Frei's son Steven, a graduate of the University of Missouri at Columbia has been associated with the business since 1976.

The aesthetic philosophy of the company was expressed by Emil Frei, Jr. when he wrote in 1950: "We are not conscious of working in a modern idiom and we never do the things we do because of a desire for *newness* ... Art must be alive and must be constantly searching to renew itself. The road therefore is upward and forward not being concerned with what those who are not initiated will accept but with what is good and right."[4] The Frei aesthetic is carried out and can be seen in a number of Chicago churches.

Wedding at Cana. *St. Ignatius Church, 6559 North Glenwood Avenue. Emil Frei Associates, St. Louis, Missouri, c. 1917. Width, 6½ feet.*

In 1917 the studio designed four large windows on either side of the nave and in 1919 two huge commemorative windows in the transepts of St. Ignatius Church. Although Frei was trained in the German Baroque style, he designed the windows at St. Ignatius to match the church's Renaissance architecture. For example, the masterfully painted *Wedding at Cana* window, modeled after an Italian painting, is a serene study in which only the ribbon work at the top of the composition and the ornate frame are in the Baroque style.

Several years later at K.A.M.—Isaiah Israel Temple, a Neo-Byzantine structure, Frei filled the window openings on seven sides of the octagonal auditorium with Judaic symbols set in clear glass bordered with simple floral designs. The window ornament is thoroughly coordinated with other decoration in the synagogue, some of which was inspired by a second century synagogue that was discovered in Tiberias in Palestine while the plan for the temple was still being developed.

For St. Viator's Church, a Neo-Gothic edifice constructed in the late 1920s, Frei again turned his attention to what is "good and right." Working in the medieval style of the thirteenth and fourteenth centuries, the studio designed row after row of medallions in rich red and blue antique glass arranged in a story-telling sequence for the tall double lancets around the church. The apse windows depict Eucharistic themes and saints associated with the Last Supper. The windows on the west side of the nave present scenes from the Old Testament and those on the east side events from the New Testament. The east transept window shows souls being released from purgatory while the west window honors the Virgin Mary with her many attributes.

For the seven large panels which comprise the huge window in the west wall of the spacious modern library of St. Xavier College, built in the 1960s, Frei Associates chose faceted slab glass. Entitled *The Spirit Will Teach All Things,* the window is filled with abstract symbols of literature, science, philosophy, and religion. The great sweeps of shimmering color integrate the panels and draw the eye irresistibly across the splendid panorama of learning.

Left:

The Spirit Will Teach You All Things. *St. Xavier College Library, 3700 West 103rd Street. Emil Frei Associates, St. Louis, 1967. Width, 24 feet.*

Right:

Moses receiving the tablets of the law, *detail of medallion windows. St. Viator Church, 4170 West Addison Street. Emil Frei Associates, St. Louis, c. 1929. Width of detail, 2 feet.*

Conrad Pickel Studio

When Conrad Pickel came to the United States in the 1930s, he had already completed eight years of formal art studies in Munich, Germany and an equal number of years as an apprentice with the Franz Mayer Company of the same city. In the United States Pickel worked for a number of prominent firms before establishing his own studio in New Berlin, Wisconsin in the mid- 1940s and a branch in Vero Beach, Florida in the 1950s. Pickel closed the Wisconsin operation in the early 1970s and moved to Florida, where his son Paul directs the Vero Beach studio while the elder Pickel experiments with new ideas in stained glass at the Gallery Fantasia, a combined art studio and workshop he built at nearby Boynton Beach.

In the early 1960s Conrad Pickel designed a large triptych which occupies the entire east wall of the modern Chapel of the Mercy Girls Home on Longwood Drive. The subject of the window is *Christ as King* interpreted in the modern spirit and with appealing simplicity. The center panel shows a large frontal figure of Christ robed in shimmering white with arms outstretched. Above and behind him stands the Virgin Mary whose voluminous blue cape envelopes him. Below Christ is a small steepled church set amidst skyscrapers of a modern city. Around the central figures and coming into the picture from the panels at either side are people from all walks of life in both ancient and modern garb, worshipers who integrate time and space into a continuity of eternal faith as they focus their attention on Christ and Mary.

Unique among the productions of the Conrad Pickel Studio, and indeed unique in all the world, is the *Salvation History* window at the Resurrection Mausoleum in Justice, Illinois, a southwest suburb of Chicago. The window covers nearly 23,000 square feet, and according to the *Guinness Book of World Records* of 1976, is the largest stained glass window in the world. A continuous wall of glass 40 feet high and 600 feet long, the window consists of 2248 panels made from 120 tons of faceted slab glass and 4000 gallons of epoxy resin. It wraps completely around the upper two stories of the mausoleum and took four years to complete from the first sketch to its installation in 1971.

Mary, Mother of Christ and of the Church. *Center panel of triptych, east wall of chapel. Mercy Girls Home, 11600 South Longwood Drive. Conrad Pickel Studios, Vero Beach, Florida, 1962. Width of center panel, 15 feet.*

The subject of the monumental project shows God at work among people from the time of Creation, through the Old and New Testaments, from Pentecost, through the Christian era and up to modern times, and concludes with the Second Coming of Christ.

The iconography of the window originated with Geoffrey Melcher, then general manager of the studio and a long-time student of biblical history. Melcher envisioned the project not so much as a biblical history but more as a portrayal of the relationship between God and humankind. Gabriel Cartwright, a staff artist of the studio and a student of the University of Wisconsin and the Layton School of Art, was assigned the enormous task of designing the window. Each panel is a work of art unto itself but is unified into the larger conception by sweeping bands and abstract forms of the same or closely related colors. Great size of itself does not necessarily constitute great art, but the *Salvation History* approaches it in the magnitude of its theme and its impeccable execution.

Left:

King David *panel, History of Salvation glass murals. Resurrection Cemetery Mausoleum, 7200 Archer Road, Justice, Illinois. Conrad Pickel Studios, Vero Beach, Florida, 1971. Width of each panel, 18 feet.*

Right:

Second Coming of Christ *panel, History of Salvation glass murals. Resurrection Cemetery Mausoleum, Conrad Pickel Studios, 1971. Width, 18 feet.*

Gabriel Loire Studio

Known throughout the world for his magnificent slab glass windows, Gabriel Loire has been called "the modern master of sculptured glass" and a "living legend" in his chosen field. Loire was born in Angers, France in 1904 and studied painting with the eminent artist Georges Rouault, one of the masters of modern stained glass art. Like many painters before him, Loire decided to make stained glass his life's work when he saw the windows at Chartres Cathedral. Soon afterward he apprenticed himself to a studio which was restoring the windows of the great cathedral.

Loire first saw slab glass at a religious art exhibit in Paris in 1927. Enthralled with its brilliance and depth of color he declared: "This was the glass of our time—the only glass I wanted to use." He experimented with the new material for years and in the shadow of Chartres opened his own studio in 1946. He then set out to look for work in French churches which had been bombed during World War II. By the end of the first year, he had made stained glass windows for thirteen churches. By 1969 he was internationally recognized and had installations in nearly 500 French churches; over 200 in the United States in both religious and secular buildings; and hundreds more in eighteen other countries as far ranging as Australia, Brazil, and Japan. In the Chicago area Loire has major installations in seven churches.

St. Thomas More Church, erected in 1958 in the modern style, has sixteen Loire windows in the elliptically-shaped clerestory. These portray events in the life of Thomas More from the time he was a lawyer and friend of King Henry VIII to his appointment as lord chancellor of England, his refusal to sign the oath which recognized Henry as the head of the church, and his subsequent imprisonment and execution. Slab glass panels in purely abstract designs also decorate both sides of the auditorium and baptistry.

In 1962 Loire completed two uninterrupted walls of glass for the newly erected St. Mark Church designed in the contemporary style. Each wall consists of six 24 by 18-foot windows principally in blue accented with brilliant flashes of red, orange, gold, green, and purple. The semi-abstract designs are symbolic of episodes in the Old and New Testaments.

Starting on the east wall of the church are the Creation of the world with God's hand over day and night, the story of Adam and Eve, Moses leading the Jews out of Egypt, the column of fire, a huge broken chain symbolizing the Jews' release from bondage, and the darkness over the earth before Christ's arrival.

Thomas More in Prison. *St. Thomas More Church, 2825 West 81st Street. Gabriel Loire Studios, Chartres, France, 1958. Width, c. 3 feet.*

The windows of the north wall begin with brilliant colors symbolic of the Redemption. The next three contain a great dove, the Holy Spirit, whose wings overshadow and protect the city of Jerusalem. The next window carries a fragment of the cross which symbolizes the saving death and resurrection of Jesus. Further on the scales of justice represent the Last Judgment. The final window announces in Hebraic script: "Hear, O Israel, the Lord our God, the Lord is One." This is followed by a brilliantly colored Greek Chi Rho and the Alpha and Omega representing Christ as the beginning and end of all things.

In an entirely different vein are the pictorial windows of medieval times which Loire designed for St. Richard's Episcopal Church in 1965. These windows of gorgeous coloration deal with important events in the dynamic thirteenth century and the personages who played key roles in shaping it.

More than forty panels decorate the nave, the baptistry, and the small chapel. The baptistry windows in the north wall are devoted to Richard as a student at Oxford, as an outcast, as the honored bishop of Chichester, and as a friend of the people and the king.

In the nave windows are the pious Louis IX of France and King Richard the Lionhearted leading a crusade to the Holy Land. Pope Innocent III is shown deposing Otto IV, emperor of the Holy Roman Empire, and Pedro of Spain. The martyrdom of Thomas à Becket is pictured together with people of high and low degree who gather at his shrine.

St. Francis of Assisi is shown with St. Clare. The great philosophers and teachers—St. Thomas Aquinas, Duns Scotus, Robert Grosseteste, Roger Bacon, and Bonaventura—are included in the sweeping panorama along with the intrepid adventurers Marco Polo and John of Monte Corvino. One of the windows is devoted to the age of building and learning and pictures Chartres Cathedral, a stained glass window, a noblewoman, and a scribe composing a letter. In the small chapel to the left of the altar are small lights of our Lady of Walsingham and the Virgin Mary with the child Jesus.

In 1966 Loire created two grand, semi-abstract windows, each 12 by 30 feet, for the sanctuary of the Immaculate Conception Church in Highland Park, Illinois. The east window, entitled the *Resurrection,* pictures Christ robed in a rich red and blue tunic and haloed by brilliant rays of white, orange, and gold. As Christ ascends to enter the glory of God, he leaves behind him the symbols of flesh and blood, here defined as a shaft of yellow wheat and clusters of blue and white grapes.

The west window, the *Immaculate Conception,* in contrast to the brilliant *Resurrection* window, is a serene study of the Virgin Mary who appears amid whorls of white and blue as if emerging from swirling clouds. White and gold stars dot the sky and the small accents of red and yellow on either side of her symbolize the earth. A single fleur-de-lis in radiant white suspended in front of Mary signifies both her purity and the light which unites her with God.

Abraham Rattner Window

The distinguished American artist Abraham Rattner (1895-1978) had always wanted to make a stained glass window. Indeed, when he received the commission for Chicago's Loop Synagogue in 1957 he had, as early as 1940, made drawings of Judeo-Christian themes with stained glass in mind.

Rattner was an intense man with a passion for perfection. Upon receiving the commission for the Loop Synagogue, he made an intensive study of Judaic liturgy and innumerable preliminary sketches of his conception. In Paris he worked with Jean Barillet, one of the world's leading glass fabricators, drawing cartoons, choosing and assembling the glass, and even climbing ladders to hold pieces of glass against the light to determine the placement of colors.

When the window was installed in 1960, just before the High Holy Days, it must have been an overwhelming experience for the congregation who first viewed it, as it is for worshipers and visitors today. The monumental window (40 by 30 feet) constitutes the entire east wall of the small sanctuary and is composed of hundreds of pieces of antique glass predominantly in ultramarine, cobalt, and cerulean blue.

Rattner was fond of double meanings and the window, entitled *And God Said, Let There Be Light And There Was Light,* can be interpreted in more ways than one. On one level it refers to the light of God's universe; on another, to the enlightenment bestowed on those of the faith through its ancient symbols; and finally to the celebration of light as it streams through the constantly changing colors, which themselves have symbolic meaning. Green signifies youth; violet, wisdom and old age; blue, the regeneration of the spirit; gold, prophecy; red, fire and creative power; and white, eternity.

At the extreme left, the focal point of the entire composition, is a brilliant gold shield and star of David encompassed by symbols of the twelve tribes of Israel. Below, in flames of red and blue, is the burning bush. At the center is a huge tree of life topped by a jeweled menorah, the seven-branched candlestick symbolic of the light of God. Other ancient symbols are the citron and the palm, representing the bounties of harvest time; and the shofar, the ram's horn sounded to call the faithful together at the High Holy Days. At the extreme right is the sun surrounded by the seven planets, and another star of David, all hurtling through God's firmament. Running across the bottom of the entire window is a wide border of faceted red and gold slab glass proclaiming in Hebrew the sacred message: "Hear, O Israel, the Lord Our God, the Lord is One."

Let There Be Light And There Was Light, *east wall. Chicago Loop Synagogue, 16 South Clark Street. Designed by Abraham Rattner, executed by Barillet Studios, Paris, France, 1960. Width, 40 feet.*

Marc Chagall at the Art Institute

The internationally acclaimed painter Marc Chagall was born in Vitebsk, Russia in 1889, but has lived most of his artistic life in France. In 1957, long after his stature as an artist was assured, Chagall received his first commission for two stained glass windows for the church at Assy. Shortly thereafter, he created two windows for the cathedral at Metz in collaboration with Charles Marq of the Atelier Jacques Simon of Reims, a partnership which has continued over the years.

Subsequent to the installation of the Metz windows, Chagall received commissions throughout Europe, in the United States, and in Israel for the renowned *Twelve Tribes of Israel* at the synagogue of the Hebrew University Medical Center in Jerusalem. In 1977 he created the *American Windows* for the Art Institute of Chicago.

Chagall always carries his mature painting style into his stained glass. Jean Leymarie says that with glass the artist has the "magical ability to animate the material and transform it into light," and the keen eye to develop "infinite nuances dominated by a single color." As in his paintings, Chagall presents elements of reality combined with mysticism, a visionary outlook, and a fantastic imagery of human forms and objects whirling in space in defiance of the laws of gravity.

The *American Windows* combine all the elements characteristic of Chagall's style. The windows are chiefly in shades of blue punctuated with flashes of red, gold, green, orange, and purple, and are divided into six panels devoted to the arts and patriotism. In the panels are typical Chagall whimsies such as tilting skyscrapers, a hand holding a flowering pen, an upside-down dancer floating in space, a small actor holding an enormous candelabra, a whirling disc symbolizing creative energy, and a music stand in mid-air. The windows face east in an area of the Art Institute dedicated to Chagall.

Chagall's *American Windows* indicate yet another direction for the use of stained glass in secular settings. It is possible that for the first time stained glass expressly created for a museum will be universally accepted on an equal plane with painting and sculpture to be viewed by the general public for its aesthetic value alone, totally divorced from its traditional role as the "handmaiden of architecture."

Immaculate Conception *window. Immaculate Conception Church, 1035 Green Bay Road, Highland Park, Illinois. Gabriel Loire Studios, Chartres, France, 1966. Width, 11 feet.*

Note: legal requirements prohibit the photographic reproduction of the Chagall American Windows *at the Art Institute.*

Notes

Chapter One

1. Coulton, G. G. *Art and the Reformation*. London: Oxford University Press, 1928, p. 339. There is no better assembly of medieval primary source material than Coulton's monumental collection. For an engaging and well-rounded secondary source with references to stained glass windows see Morris Bishop's *The Middle Ages,* American Heritage Press: 1970.

2. As quoted in Gardner, Helen. *Art Through the Ages.* New York: Harcourt Brace & Co., 1948, p. 360. Gardner's splendid study is essentially an overview. For a greater in-depth study of Gothic architecture see Louis Grodecki's Gothic Architecture. New York: Harry N. Abrams, Inc., 1977.

3. Adams, Henry. *Mont-St.-Michel and Chartres.* New York: Doubleday & Co., 1933, p. 152. A romantic, personal, solidly written essay, not only on the windows at Chartres, which Adams visited with glassman John La Farge, but on the entire panorama of life and thinking in the thirteenth century.

4. Sowers, Robert. "Stained Glass," *New Catholic Encyclopedia,* vol. XIII. New York: McGraw-Hill Book Co., 1967, p. 630. Sowers' *Stained Glass an Architectural Art* should be read for his in-depth and erudite discussion of the aesthetic and technical problems peculiar to stained glass art.

5. Lee, Lawrence, et. al. *Stained Glass.* New York: Crown Publishers, Inc., 1976. One of the best overviews of recent stained glass publications.

6. Rigan, Otto B. *New Glass.* San Francisco: San Francisco Book Company, Inc., 1976, p. 93. Kehlmann in a letter to the authors dated May 22, 1982, states that he prefers the term "non-architectural" to "autonomous." We have therefore made the substitution to accord with his revised thinking.

Chapter Two

1. As quoted in Koch, Robert. *Louis C. Tiffany: Rebel in Glass.* New York: Crown Publishers, Inc., 1964, p. 55.

2. As quoted in Johnson, Diane C. *American Art Nouveau.* New York: Harry N. Abrams, Inc., 1979, p. 78.

3; As quoted in Hanks, David A. *The Decorative Designs of Frank Lloyd Wright.* New York: E. P. Dutton, 1979, p. 56.

4. *Arts For America.* vol. 5 (March, 1886), p. 67.

5. As quoted in Lynes, Russell. *The Tastemakers.* New York: Harper Brothers, 1954, pp. 95-96.

6. *Industrial Chicago: The Building Interests.* vol. 2. Chicago: Goodspeed Publishing Co., 1891, p. 490.

7. Wright, Frank Lloyd. *An Autobiography.* New York: Duell, Sloan and Pearce, 1943, p. 155.

8. "Three Newly Completed Stained Glass Windows Depicting The Patriarchs." Pamphlet published by Temple Sholom, 1982.

9. As quoted in Darling, Sharon. *Chicago Ceramics and Glass.* Chicago: Chicago Historical Society, 1979, p. 154.

10. As quoted in Kaufmann, Edgar and Raeburn, Ben. *Frank Lloyd Wright, Writings and Buildings.* New York: Horizon Press, 1960, p. 227.

Chapter Three

1. Koch, Robert. *Louis Comfort Tiffany 1848-1933.* New York: Museum of Contemporary Crafts, 1958, p. 8.

2. As quoted in Amaya, Mario. *Tiffany Glass.* New York: Walker and Company, 1967, p. 29.

3. Sturm, James L. *Stained Glass from Medieval Times to the Present: Treasures to Be Seen in New York.* New York: E. P. Dutton, Inc., 1982, p. 32.

4. Frei, Emil, "Emil Frei on Modern Glass." *Stained Glass.* 62, No. 3 (Autumn, 1967), p. 47.

5. Leymarie, Jean. *Marc Chagall: The Jerusalem Windows.* New York: George Braziller, 1962, p. 17.

Bibliography

Books

Adams, Henry. *Mont-St.-Michel and Chartres.* New York: Doubleday & Co., 1933.

Amayo, Mario. *Tiffany Glass.* New York: Walker & Co., 1967.

Andreas, A. T. *History of Chicago from the Earliest Period to the Present.* 3 vols. Chicago: A. T. Andreas, 1884-1886.

Arnold, Hugh. *Stained Glass of the Middle Ages in England.* London: Adam and Charles Black, 1939.

Barr, Alfred H. Jr. *Matisse His Art and His Public.* New York: Museum of Modern Art, 1951.

Battersby, Martin. *The Decorative Twenties.* New York: Walker & Co., 1951.

_____. *The Decorative Thirties.* New York: Walker & Co., 1970.

Bing, Samuel. *Artistic America, Tiffany Glass and Art Nouveau.* Cambridge, Mass.: MIT Press, 1970.

Bishop, Morris. *The Middle Ages.* New York: American Heritage Press, 1970.

Blake, Peter. *The Master Builders Le Corbusier, Mies van der Rohe and Frank Lloyd Wright.* New York: Alfred A. Knopf, 1960.

Burg, David A. *Chicago's White City.* Lexington, Ky.: University of Kentucky Press, 1976.

Carter, Thomas. *The Second Presbyterian Church, 1842-1892.* Chicago: Knight, Leonard & Co., 1892.

Chicago and the World's Fair of 1933. Chicago: F. Husum Publishing Co., 1933.

Chicago Landmarks 1978. Chicago: Commission on Chicago Historical and Architectural Landmarks, 1978.

City Blue Book of Biography. Chicago: Clark J. Heringshaw, 1920-1930.

City Directories of Chicago. Chicago: various publishers, 1850-1917; 1923; 1928-29.

Clark, Robert Judson (ed.). *The Arts and Crafts Movement in America, 1876-1916.* Princeton, N.J.: Princeton University Press, 1972.

Conant, Kenneth John. *Carolingian and Romanesque Architecture.* Hammondsworth, Middlesex, England: Penguin Books, Ltd. 1966.

Condit, Paul. *The Chicago School of Architecture.* Chicago: University of Chicago Press, 1964.

Connick, Charles J. *Adventures in Light and Color.* New York: Random House, 1937.

Coulton, G. G. *Art and the Reformation.* London: Oxford University Press, 1928.

Cowen, Painton. *Rose Windows.* San Francisco: Chronicle Books, 1979.

Darling, Sharon S. *Chicago Ceramics and Glass, 1871-1933.* Chicago: Chicago Historical Society, 1979.

de Breffny, Brian. *The Synagogue.* New York: Macmillan Publishing Co., Inc., 1978.

Department of Development and Planning. *Historic City: The Settlement of Chicago.* Chicago: City of Chicago, 1976.

Dierick, Alfons. *The Stained Glass at Chartres.* Berne: Hallwag Ltd., 1960.

Duncan, Alastair. *Tiffany Windows.* New York: Simon & Schuster, 1980.

Frueh, Erne R. and Frueh, Florence. *The Second Presbyterian Church of Chicago, Art and Architecture.* Chicago: Second Presbyterian Church, 1976.

Gardner, Helen. *Art Through the Ages.* New York: Harcourt Brace & Co., 1948.

Gilbert, Paul and Bryson, Charles Lee. *Chicago and Its Makers.* Chicago: Felix Mendelsohn Publisher, 1929.

Grodecki, Louis. *Gothic Architecture.* New York: Harry N. Abrams, Inc., 1977.

Hanks, David A. *The Decorative Designs of Frank Lloyd Wright.* New York: E. P. Dutton, 1979.

Hawthorne, John G. and Smith, Cyril Stanley. *On the Divers Arts. The Treatise of Theophilus.* Translated from the Medieval Latin with an introduction and notes by John G. Hawthorne and Cyril Stanley Smith. Chicago: University of Chicago Press, 1963.

Hilton, Timothy. *The Pre-Raphaelites.* New York: Harry N. Abrams, Inc., 1970.

Horowitz, Helen Lefkowitz. *Culture and the City.* Lexington, Ky.: University of Kentucky Press, 1976.

Husband, Joseph. *The Story of the Pullman Palace Car.* Chicago: A. C. McClurg & Co., 1917.

Industrial Chicago: The Building Interests. 2 vols. Chicago: Goodspeed Publishing Co., 1891-96.

Isenberg, Anita and Isenberg, Seymour. *How to Work in Stained Glass.* Radnor, Pa.: Chilton Book Co., 1972.

Bibliography *continued*

Johnson, Diane C. *American Art Nouveau.* New York: Harry N. Abrams, Inc., 1979.

Kampf, Avram. *Contemporary Synagogue Art.* New York: Union of American Hebrew Congregations, 1966.

Kaufmann, Edgar and Raeburn, Ben. (eds.). *Frank Lloyd Wright: Writings and Buildings.* New York: Horizon Press, 1960.

Koch, Robert. *Louis C. Tiffany, 1848-1933.* New York: Museum of Contemporary Crafts, 1958.

_____. *Louis C. Tiffany Rebel in Glass.* New York: Crown Publishers, 1964.

Kunstler, Gustav. *Romanesque Architecture in Europe.* New York: W. W. Norton & Co., 1973.

Lane, George A. *Chicago Churches and Synagogues.* Chicago: Loyola University Press, 1981.

Lawrence, Lee; Seddon, George, and Stephens, Frank. *Stained Glass.* New York: Crown Publishers, 1976.

Le Couteur, J. D. *English Medieval Painted Glass.* New York: Macmillan Co. 1926.

Leepa, Allen. *Abraham Rattner.* New York: Harry N. Abrams, Inc., 1974.

Leymarie, Jean. *Marc Chagall: The Jerusalem Windows.* New York: George Braziller, 1962.

Lowe, David. *Chicago Interiors.* Chicago: Contemporary Books, Inc., 1979.

_____. *Lost Chicago.* Boston: Houghton Mifflin Co., 1975.

Lynes, Russell. *The Tastemakers.* New York: Harper & Brothers, 1954.

McKay, Charles (anon. author). *The Art Work of Louis C. Tiffany.* New York: Doubleday Page, 1914.

Male, Emile. *The Early Churches of Rome.* Chicago: Quadrangle Books, Inc., 1960.

Manson, Grant Carpenter. *Frank Lloyd Wright to 1910.* New York: Van Nostrand Reinhold Co., 1958.

Marquis, Albert Nelson (ed.). *The Book of Chicagoans.* Chicago: A. N. Marquis & Co., 1917-1933.

Marteau, Robert. *The Stained Glass Windows of Chagall.* New York: Tudor Publishing Co., 1973.

Morris, William. *The Letters of William Morris to His Friends and Family.* (Philip Henderson, ed.). New York: Longmans Green & Co., 1950.

Morrison, Hugh. *Louis Sullivan Prophet of Modern Architecture.* New York: W. W. Norton & Co., 1935.

Mucha, Jiri. *Alphonse Mucha.* Prague: Knibtisk Arta. 1966.

Muller, Robert. *Uses of the Past.* New York: Oxford University Press, 1957.

Otis, Philo Adams. *The First Presbyterian Church.* Chicago: F. Summy Co., 1900.

Overy, Paul. *De Stijl.* London: Studio Vista, 1969.

Panofsky, Erwin. "Abbot Suger of St. Denis." In *Meaning of the Visual Arts.* New York: Doubleday Anchor Books, 1955.

Peguy, Charles. *Le Monde de Chartres.* Paris: Zodiaque, 1961.

Pevsner, Nikolaus. *Pioneers of Modern Design from William Morris to Walter Gropius.* Hammondsworth, Middlesex, England: Penguin Books, 1960.

Pierce, Bessie Louise. *A History of Chicago.* 3 vols. New York: Alfred A. Knopf, 1937-57.

Piper, John. *Stained Glass Art or Anti-Art.* London: Studio Vista, 1968.

Poole, Ernest. *Giants Gone: The Men Who Made Chicago.* New York: Whittlesey House, 1943.

Ralph, Julian. *Chicago and the World's Fair.* New York: Harper & Brothers, 1893.

Randall, Frank. *A History of the Development of Building Construction in Chicago.* Urbana, Ill.: University of Illinois Press, 1949.

Reyntiens, Patrick. *The Technique of Stained Glass.* New York: Watson-Guptill Publications, 1967.

Rice, David Talbot. *Art of the Byzantine Era.* New York: Frederick A. Praeger Publishers, 1963.

Rigan, Otto. *New Glass.* San Francisco: San Francisco Book Co., 1976.

Rheims, Maurice. *L'Art 1900.* Paris: Arts et Meters Graphiques, 1965.

Rogers, Frances and Beard, Alice. *5000 Years of Glass.* New York: Frederick A. Stokes Co., 1937.

Sewter, A. Charles. *The Stained Glass of William Morris and His Circle.* 2 vols. New York: Yale University Press, 1974.

Sowers, Robert. *The Lost Art: A Survey of 5000 Years of Stained Glass.* New York: George A. Wittenborn, Inc., 1956.

_____. *Stained Glass an Architectural Art.* New York: Universe Books, Inc. 1965.

Spencer, Robin. *The Aesthetic Movement.* London: Studio Vista, 1972.

Sturm, James L. *Stained Glass from Medieval Times to the Present, Treasures to Be Seen in New York.* New York: E. P. Dutton, Inc., 1982.

Suger, Abbot. *On the Abbey Church of St. Denis and Its Treasures.* (Erwin Panofsky and Gerda Panofsky-Soergel eds.). Princeton, N.J.: Princeton University Press, 1979.

Sullivan, Louis H. *The Autobiography of an Idea.* New York: American Institute of Architects, 1924.

_____ . *Kindergarten Chats and Other Writings.* (Isabella Athey, ed.). New York: George A. Wittenborn, Inc., 1947.

Tallmadge, Thomas E. *Architecture in Old Chicago.* Chicago: University of Chicago Press, 1941.

Thompson, Joseph J. *The Archdiocese of Chicago.* Chicago: St. Mary's Press, 1920.

Thompson, Paul. *The Work of William Morris.* New York: Viking Press, 1967.

Tiffany Studios. *A Partial List of Windows.* New York: Tiffany Studios, 1910.

Vinci, John. *The Art Institute of Chicago: The Stock Exchange Trading Room.* Chicago: The Art Institute of Chicago, 1977.

Wagenknecht, Edward. *Chicago.* Norman, Okla.: University of Oklahoma Press, 1964.

Wright, Frank Lloyd. *An Autobiography.* New York: Duell, Sloan and Pearce, 1943.

Periodicals

Adams, Henry B. "The Stained Glass of John La Farge." *American Art Review* (July-August, 1975).

Arts for America. Various issues, 1897-1904.

Brush and Pencil. Various issues, 1896-1917.

Field Museum of Natural History. *Bulletin* (June, 1978).

Frei, Emil. "Emil Frei on Modern Glass." *Stained Glass* 62, no. 3 (Autumn, 1967).

Frueh, Erne R. and Frueh, Florence. "The Ivanhoe Window." *Stained Glass* 77, no. 2 (Summer, 1982).

_____ . "Munich Studio Windows at SS. Cyril and Methodius Church." *Stained Glass* 74, no. 2 (Summer, 1979).

_____ . "St. Cecilia in Chicago." *Stained Glass* 76, no. 1 (Spring, 1981).

The Glassworker. Various issues 1902-1915.

Hanks, David A. "Louis J. Millet and the Art Institute of Chicago." *Bulletin of the Art Institute of Chicago* (March-April, 1973).

Inland Architect and Builder. Various issues, 1898-1924.

Low, Will H. "Old Glass in New Windows." *Scribner's Magazine* 4 (1888).

Nelson, Susan. "Mr. White's Remarkable Glass Works." *Chicago Tribune Sunday Magazine,* April 2, 1970.

Ross, Walter. "Stained Glass by a Modern Master." *Reader's Digest* (December, 1969).

Skinner, Orin E. "Connick in Retrospect." *Stained Glass* 70, no. 1 (Spring, 1975).

Sowers, Robert. "Learning to Speak the Language of Stained Glass." *Stained Glass* 75, no. 4 (Winter, 1980-81).

Taolin, Anna. "The World's Largest Stained Glass Window." *Stained Glass* 72, no. 2 (Summer, 1977).

Temme, Norman. "Charles Z. Lawrence . . . A Twenty Year Dream Come True." *Stained Glass* 74, no. 4 (Winter, 1979-80).

Tiffany, Louis C. "American Art Supreme in Colored Glass." *The Forum* 15 (1893).

_____ . "Color and Its Kinship to Sound." *The Art World* 2 (1917).

_____ . "The Quest for Beauty." *Harpers Bazaar* (December, 1917).

Viollet-le-Duc, Eugene. "Vitrail." *Dictionnaire Raisoné de l'Architecture Francais* (republished as a series). *Stained Glass* 26, 27 (1931-32).

von Roenn, Kenneth. "The Development of Contemporary German Stained Glass and Its Influence on American Artists." *New Work* (Winter, 1982).

Weinberg, Helene Barbara. "The Early Stained Glass Work of John La Farge." *Stained Glass* 67, no. 2 (Summer, 1972).

_____ . "John La Farge and the Invention of American Opalescent Windows." *Stained Glass* 67, no. 3 (Autumn, 1972).

Weis, Helene. "Iconography Can Be Contemporary." *Stained Glass* 77, no. 4 (Winter 1982-83).

Willett, Henry Lee. "Henry Lee Willett, Troublesome Fellow." *Stained Glass* 73, no. 1 (Spring, 1978).

Bibliography *continued*

Booklets and Pamphlets

Bletzer, Russell. "The Fused Glass Windows of the North Shore Unitarian Church." Explains iconography of artist Bob White's work.

"Building Our Future Together." First Presbyterian Church, Lake Forest, Illinois. Colored illustrations and installation dates of the church's Tiffany windows.

Frei, Emil. "The Windows at St. Viator's Church." Frei discusses in depth his concept of the medieval windows he designed for this church.

"Immaculate Conception Church: Dedication, April, 1967." Explains the symbolism of the *Resurrection* and *Immaculate Conception* windows by Loire.

Kretzmann, Adalbert R. "The Evangelical Lutheran Church of St. Luke." Explains the symbolism of Giannini & Hilgart's abstract window behind the altar.

"The Partiarchs." Interesting discussion by artist Archie Rand and of his designs for three patriarch windows at Temple Sholom.

Melcher, Geoffrey (anon. author). "Salvation History. The Glass Murals of Resurrection Mausoleum." A detailed explanation of the iconography of the largest stained glass window in the world.

"St. Mark Dedication Book." (March 17, 1967). Contains a lengthy discussion of Gabriel Loire's iconography of events from the Old and New Testaments.

Schloerb, Rolland Walter. "Our House of Worship." Hyde Park Union Church. Written as a guided tour of the church with emphasis on the church's windows by Connick, Tiffany, and Zettler.

"That We May Have Preists." Quigley Seminary South. Describes artist Max Ingrand's windows in the chapel.

"Windows at St. Richard's Episcopal Church." (mimeographed, 1962). Contains diagrams pertinent to Loire's studies of St. Richard and his times.

Interviews

Corbin, Craig. Owner Mountain Lights Glass Co., Highland Park, Ill. Discussion on autonomous stained glass art, April, 1982.

Drehobl, Frank J. Jr. President Drehobl Bros. Art Glass Co. Conversations about past Chicago glassmen. August, 1979; September, 1980; March, 1982.

Morlock, A. Owner of Chicago's most extensive collection of secular Victorian windows displayed at his Victorian House Restaurant. February, 1983.

O'Shaughnessy, Joseph. Son of the stained glass artist Thomas Augustin O'Shaughnessy. Various dates (1981-82).

Snyder, Thomas. Master glass painter for the Drehobl Bros. Art Glass Co. Demonstration and discussion on painting techniques. March, 1982.

Valeska, Adolfas. Owner of the Valeska Art Studio. Visit to the shop and demonstration by Valeska on his use of slab glass and epoxy resin. February, 1983.

Wandzura, Lubomyr. President of Giannini & Hilgart. Discussion on French and German antique glass. December, 1982.

White, Bob. Conversation with the artist on his fused glass technique. March, 1983.

Archives and Memorabilia

Drehobl Bros. Art Glass Co. Archives.

Giannini & Hilgart. Archives.

O'Shaughnessy, Joseph. Memorabilia of Thomas Augustin O'Shaughnessy.

Valeska Art Studio. Archives.

Studios and Installations

Stained glass studios and their Chicago installations. Chicago firms unless otherwise noted. Addresses indicate the fronts of buildings.

Artmaier, Joseph
St. Mary of Perpetual Help Church
1035 West 32nd Street

St. George Church
902 West 33rd Street

Atelier Jacques Simon   Reims, France
The Art Institute of Chicago
   (American windows designed by Marc Chagall)
Michigan Avenue at Adams Street

Baransky Studios   Yonkers, New York
SS. Volodymyr and Olha Church
739 North Oakley Boulevard   (2300 West)

Barillet Studio   Paris, France
Chicago Loop Synagogue
   (window designed by Abraham Rattner)
16 South Clark Street   (100 West)

Botti Studios of Architectural Arts
Evanston, Illinois
Apostolic Church of God
6303 South Kenwood Avenue (1342 East)

St. Gregory the Illuminator Church
6700 West Diversey Boulevard (2800 North)

Life Center Church of Universal Awareness
55th and Indiana Avenue (200 East)

Queen of Heaven Cemetery Mausoleum
1400 South Wolf Road
Hillside, Illinois

St. Thomas Episcopal Church
3801 South Wabash Avenue (50 East)

Clinton Glass Company   (1897-1962)
Blessed Agnes Church
2655 South Central Park Avenue   (3600 West)

Our Lady of Sorrows Basilica   (north facade windows)
3101 West Jackson Boulevard   (300 South)

Connick Associates   (1912-   )
Boston, Massachusetts
Blair Chapel, Fourth Presbyterian Church   (west wall)
876 North Michigan Avenue   (100 East)

Bond Chapel
1050 East 59th Street

St. Chrysostom's Church
1424 North Dearborn Parkway   (50 West)

First Unitarian Church of Chicago
   (small rose window)
5650 South Woodlawn Avenue   (1200 East)

Fourth Presbyterian Church
876 North Michigan Avenue   (100 East)

Hyde Park Union Church
5600 South Woodlawn Avenue   (1200 East)

St. James Episcopal Cathedral
   (Randall memorial window)
65 East Huron Street   (700 North)

Presbyterian Church   (one window right side of altar)
Deerpath and Sheridan Roads
Lake Forest, Illinois

Daprato Rigali   Franklin Park, Illinois
Christ the King Church
9235 South Hamilton Avenue   (2132 West)

St. Constance Church
5843 West Strong Street   (4932 North)

St. Cornelius Church
5205 North Lieb Avenue   (5424 West)

St. Felicitas Church
1526 East 84th Street

St. Ferdinand Church
5900 West Barry Avenue   (3100 North)

St. Gabriel Church
4501 South Lowe Avenue   (632 West)

St. John Bosco Church
2250 North McVicker Avenue   (6034 West)

St. Mary Star of the Sea Church
6435 South Kilbourn Avenue   (4500 West)

St. Priscilla Church
6969 West Addison Street   (3600 North)

Queen of Angels Church
2330 West Sunnyside Avenue   (4500 North)

Our Lady of Grace Church
2455 North Hamlin Avenue   (3800 West)

St. Tarcissus Church
6020 West Ardmore Avenue   (5800 North)

St. Catherine of Sienna Church
38 North Austin Boulevard
Oak Park, Illinois

Queen of Heaven Mausoleum
1400 South Wolf Road
Hillside, Illinois

Studios and Installations *continued*

D'Ogier Studios   New Hope, Connecticut
St. Thomas the Apostle Church
5476 South Kimbark Avenue   (1300 East)

Drehobl Brothers Art Glass Company   (1919-   )
Anshe Emet Synagogue
3760 North Pine Grove Avenue   (700 West)

Assumption B.V.M. Church   (nave windows)
319 West Illinois Street   (500 North)

Bethesda Evangelical Lutheran Church
6803 North Campbell Avenue   (2500 West)

Chatham Presbyterian Church   (chancel window)
741 East 84th Street

Edgebrook Lutheran Church   (transept windows)
5252 West Devon Avenue   (6400 North)

Felician Sisters' Infirmary Chapel
3800 West Peterson Avenue   (6000 North)

St. Gregory Convent Chapel
5520 North Paulina Avenue   (1700 West)

Immaculate Heart of Mary Church
3307 West Byron Street   (3900 North)

Irving Park United Methodist Church
3801 North Keeler Avenue   (4200 West)

St. John United Church of Christ
2442 West Moffat Street   (1834 North)

Luther Memorial Church
2500 West Wilson Avenue   (4600 North)

Ner Tamid Congregation
2754 West Rosemont Avenue   (6300 North)

North Shore Baptist Church
  (execution of jade window)
5244 North Lakewood Avenue   (1300 West)

Our Lady of Mount Carmel Chapel
690 West Belmont Avenue   (3200 North)

Pilgrim Lutheran Church
  (chancel and chapel windows)
4300 North Winchester Avenue   (1950 West)

Queen of the Universe Church
7130 South Hamlin Avenue   (3800 West)

St. Simon the Apostle Church
5157 South California Avenue   (2800 West)

Temple Shaare Tikvah
5800 North Kimball Avenue   (3400 West)

Temple Sholom   (three prophet windows)
3480 North Lake Shore Drive   (500 East)

Esser Company, T. C.   Menomonee Falls, Wisconsin
Blair Chapel
Fourth Presbyterian Church
876 North Michigan Avenue   (100 East)

Dominican Priory
7200 West Division Street
River Forest, Illinois

SS. Faith, Hope and Charity
191 Linden Street
Winnetka, Illinois

Grace Evangelical Lutheran Church
7300 West Division Street
River Forest, Illinois

St. Helen Church
2315 West Augusta Boulevard   (1000 North)

St. Odilo Church
2244 South East Avenue
Berwyn, Illinois

St. Pascal Church
3935 North Melvina Avenue   (6200 West)

Northminster Presbyterian Church of Evanston
2515 Central Park Avenue
Evanston, Illinois

Queen of All Saints Basilica
6284 North Sauganash Avenue   (4700 West)

Flanagan and Biedenweg   (1885-1952)
De Paul University   (Magi window not *in situ*)
2323 North Seminary Avenue   (1100 West)

St. Vincent de Paul Church   (transept windows)
1004 West Webster Avenue   (2200 North)

Frei Art Glass Company, Emil   (1904-   )
St. Louis, Missouri
St. Ignatius Church
6559 North Glenwood Avenue   (1400 West)

St. Jerome Church
1607 West Lunt Avenue   (7000 North)

K.A.M.—Isaiah Israel Temple
1100 East Hyde Park Boulevard   (5100 South)

St. Viator Church
4160 West Addison Street   (3600 North)

St. Xavier College Library
3700 West 103rd Street   (10300 South)

Gawin Company   Milwaukee, Wisconsin
St. John Cantius Church
821 North Carpenter Street   (1032 West)

Giannini & Hilgart (1899-   )
St. Angela Church
1306 North Massasoit Avenue (5732 West)

The Chicago Temple
First United Methodist Church
77 West Washington Street   (100 North)

Church of the Ascension
   (four south nave windows)
1133 North La Salle Street   (150 West)

Grace Lutheran Church
1430 South Boulevard
Evanston, Illinois

St. Luke Evangelical Lutheran Church
1500 West Belmont Avenue   (3200 North)

Messiah Evangelical Lutheran Church
6201 West Peterson Avenue   (6000 North)

St. Nicholas Ukrainian Catholic Cathedral
   (recent windows)
2238 West Rice Street   (824 North)

Our Lady of Grace Church
2450 North Ridgeway Avenue   (3732 West)

St. Paul's Church
2335 North Orchard Street   (700 West)

St. Sabina Church
1210 West 78th Place   (1300 West)

Hardman and Company, John   London, England
Holy Angels Church
605 East Oakwood Boulevard   (3940 South)

Healy & Millet (1880-98)
Auditorium Theatre Building
Roosevelt University
430 South Michigan Avenue   (100 East)

Pilgrim Baptist Church
3301 South Indiana Avenue   (200 East)

Ryerson Library   (skylight designed by Millet)
The Art Institute of Chicago
Michigan Avenue at Adams Street

Second Presbyterian Church
   (one window—*Cast Thy Garment . . .*)
1936 South Michigan Avenue   (100 East)

Heinigke & Bowen   New York, New York
University Club of Chicago, Cathedral Hall
   (windows designed by Frederic C. Bartlett)
76 East Monroe Street   (100 South)

Ingrand Max   Paris, France
St. Denis Church
8301 South St. Louis Avenue   (3500 West)

St. Mary of the Woods Church
7000 North Moselle Avenue   (6000 West)

St. Rita High School
7740 South Western Avenue   (2400 West)

Kevelear and Goch, W. Derix   Germany
Holy Rosary Church
351 East 113th Street

Kinsella Company, John J.   (1872-1931)
St. James Lutheran Church
2048 North Fremont Street   (900 West)

St. John Berchmans Church
2519 West Logan Boulevard   (2600 North)

St. James Chapel
Quigley Preparatory Seminary North
631 North Rush Street   (75 East)

Seminary Chapel
St. Mary of the Lake Seminary
Mundelein, Illinois

La Farge, John   (1835-1910)
New York, New York

Second Presbyterian Church   (one nave window)
1936 South Michigan Avenue   (100 East)

Lascelles & Shroeder   (active 1895-?)
Notre Dame Church
1336 West Flournoy Street   (700 South)

Our Lady of Fatima
2751 West 38th Place

Linden Glass Company   (1882-1934)
Frederick J. Robie House
5757 South Woodlawn Avenue   (1200 East)

Loire Studios, Gabriel   (1946-   )
Chartres, France

Immaculate Conception Church
1590 Green Bay Road
Highland Park, Illinois

St. John Fisher Church
   (also Conrad Schmitt windows)
10234 South Washtenaw Avenue   (2700 West)

St. Lambert Church
8148 Karlov Avenue
Skokie, Illinois   (4100 West)

Loyola Academy   (basement chapel)
1100 Laramie Avenue
Wilmette, Illinois

St. Mark Church
1048 North Campbell Avenue   (2500 West)

St. Richard Episcopal Church
5101 West Devon Avenue   (6400 North)

St. Thomas More Church
2825 West 81st Street

MacKay, Joseph Evan
United Church of Hyde Park   (Lily window)
1400 East 53rd Street

Maumejean Freres,   France
St. Ita Church
5500 North Broadway   (1200 West)

Mayer & Company   Munich, Germany
St. Alphonsus Church
2950 North Southport Avenue   (1400 West)

St. Bartholomew Church
3601 North Lavergne Avenue   (5000 West)

St. Gertrude Church
6204 North Glenwood Avenue   (1400 West)

St. Josaphat Church   (apse windows)
2301 North Southport Avenue (1400 West)

St. Michael Redemptorist Church
455 West Eugenie Street   (1700 North)

St. Vincent de Paul Church   (nave windows)
1004 West Webster Avenue   (2200 North)

McCully & Miles   (1872-1914?)
Second Presbyterian Church   (four nave windows)
1936 South Michigan Avenue   (100 East)

Michaudel Studio, Arthur   (-1945)
Church of the Atonement   (west facade and nave)
5749 North Kenmore Avenue   (1040 West)

Holy Cross Church
1736 West 46th Street

Miller, Edgar   (active 1927-60)
The Art Institute of Chicago
   (Logan Purchase Prize window)
Michigan Avenue at Adams Street

The Art Institute of Chicago   (Diana Court windows)
Michigan Avenue at Adams Street

Misch & Bro., George A.   (1864-   )
First Baptist Congregational Church
60 North Ashland Avenue   (1600 West)

Morris, William   (1861-1896)
London, England

Second Presbyterian Church   (two vestibule windows
   designed by Edward Burne-Jones, 1833-1898)
1936 South Michigan Avenue   (100 East)

Munich Studio, The   (1903-1933)
St. Bridget Church
2940 South Archer Avenue   (1500 West)

St. Dominic Church
869 North Sedgwick Street   (400 West)

St. Leo Church
7750 South Emerald Avenue   (732 West)

St. Margaret Mary School   (three vestibule windows)
2302 W. Chase Avenue   (7300 North)

St. Margaret of Scotland Church
1256 West 99th Street

St. Nicholas Ukrainian Catholic Cathedral
2238 West Rice Street   (824 North)

Our Lady of Sorrows Basilica   (choir balcony and
   transept clerestory windows. Also *Pieta* and choir
   chapel windows.)
3101 West Jackson Boulevard   (300 South)

St. Philip Lutheran Church
6232 South Eberhart Avenue   (500 East)

St. Veronica Church
3316 North Whipple Street   (3032 West)

O'Brien, Richard
St. Jane de Chantal Church
5251 South McVicker Avenue   (6024 West)

O'Duggan, John Terrance
St. Philip Neri Church
2126 East 72nd Street

O'Shaughnessy, Thomas A.   (active c. 1911-1952)
St. Benedict Chapel
Illinois Benedictine College
5700 College Road   Lisle, Illinois

Chicago Historical Society
   (one window to be received 1983)
North Avenue at Clark Street

Madonna della Strada Chapel   (sixteen small lights)
6525 North Sheridan Road   (at Lake Michigan)

Old St. Patrick's Church
140 South Desplaines Street

St. Stephen's Episcopal Church   (one window)
3533 North Albany Avenue   (3100 West)

Pickel Art Glass Studios   Vero Beach, Florida
All Saints Mausoleum
700 North River Road
Des Plaines, Illinois

St. Bede Church
8200 South Kostner   (4400 West)

Carmelite Monastery
River Road at Central
Des Plaines, Illinois

Cenacle Retreat House Chapel   (East windows)
11600 South Longwood Drive   (1826 West)

Lincolnwood Jewish Congregation
7117 North Crawford Avenue   (4000 West)

Resurrection Cemetery Mausoleum
7200 Archer Avenue
Justice, Illinois

Reynolds, Francis & Rohnstock
Boston, Massachusetts
Church of the Ascension   (west nave window)
1133 North LaSalle Drive   (150 West)

Salano Company   Milan, Italy
Holy Name Cathedral
735 North State Street

Schmitt Studios, Conrad   New Berlin, Wisconsin
Academy of Our Lady
1309 West 95th Street

St. Gall Church
5500 South Kedzie Avenue   (3200 West)

Holy Resurrection Serbian Orthodox Cathedral
5701 North Redwood Drive   (8024 West)

St. John Baptist De La Salle Church
165 East 115th Street

St. John Fisher Church   (also Loire windows)
10234 South Washtenaw Avenue   (2700 West)

St. Peter's Episcopal Church
621 West Belmont Avenue   (3200 North)

Resurrection Hospital
7435 West Talcott Road   (5400 North)

St. Vincent de Paul Church   (rose window)
1004 West Webster Avenue   (2200 North)

St. Walter's Church
11722 South Oakley Avenue   (2300 West)

St. William's Church
3600 North Sayre Avenue   (7000 West)

Shaw, Howard Van Doren   (1869-1926)
Second Presbyterian Church   (one large nave,
    many small nave and vestibule windows)
1936 South Michigan Avenue   (100 East)

Sperry, Edward Peck   (1890-   )
New York Church Glass & Decorating Company
    and Tiffany Studio, New York, New York
Armour Institute   (triptych, administration building)
Illinois Institute of Technology
10 West 33rd Street

Frank Dickinson Bartlett Memorial Gymnasium
5640 South University Avenue   (1116 East)

Temple Art Glass Company   (1903-1933)
Unity Temple
875 Lake Street at Kenilworth
Oak Park, Illinois

Tiffany Studios   (1879-1930)
New York, New York
Chicago Public Library Cultural Center
    (glass domes in Preston Bradley Hall, in G.A.R.
    foyer, and mosaics)
78 East Washington Street   (100 North)

Church of our Savior   (five nave windows)
530 West Fullerton Parkway   (2400 North)

Field Museum of Natural History
H. N. Higginbotham Hall
East Roosevelt Road and South Lake Shore Drive

Hyde Park Union Church   (four nave windows)
5600 South Woodlawn Avenue   (1200 East)

Marshall Field & Company   (favrile glass domes)
111 North State Street

Marquette Building   (mosaics in rotunda)
South Dearborn and West Adams Streets

Presbyterian Church   (four north nave windows)
Deerpath and Sheridan Roads
Lake Forest, Illinois

Rosehill Cemetery Mausoleum (many signed windows
    including John G. Shedd Memorial window,
    triptych)
5800 North Ravenswood Avenue   (1800 West)

Second Presbyterian Church   (nine nave and five
    narthex windows)
1936 South Michigan Avenue   (100 East)

Studios and Installations *continued*

Tonelli's Studio   Florence, Italy
Dan Ryan Memorial Chapel windows
St. Joseph Hospital
2900 North Lake Shore Drive   (300 East)

Tyrol Art Glass Company   Innsbruck, Austria
St. Priscilla
6969 West Addison Street   (3600 North)

St. Vincent de Paul   (small nave windows)
1004 West Webster Avenue   (2200 North)

Valeska Art Studio   (1950-   )
Cenacle Retreat House Chapel   (five west windows)
11600 South Longwood Drive   (1826 West)

Cenacle Retreat House Chapel
513 West Fullerton Parkway   (2400 North)

Nativity of the Blessed Virgin Mary Church
6812 South Washtenaw Avenue   (2700 West)

O'Hare International Airport
42nd Parallel Restaurant and Lounge windows

Palos Community Hospital Chapel
80th Avenue at McCarthy Road
Palos Heights, Illinois

St. Philomena Church   (windows and mosaics)
1921 North Kedvale Avenue   (4134 West)

Polish Jesuit Residence Chapel
4105 North Avers Avenue   (3834 West)

Rodfei Zedek Temple
5200 South Hyde Park Boulevard   (1700 East)

Von Gerichten Art Glass Company
Columbus, Ohio
Holy Family Church   (figurative windows in nave)
1080 West Roosevelt Road   (1200 South)

Wells Brothers   (1870-   )
Trinity Episcopal Church
125 East 26th Street

White, Bob   (active 1930-1982)
Holy Name of Mary Church
11159 South Loomis Street   (1400 West)

North Shore Unitarian Church
2100 Half Day Road
Deerfield, Illinois

Willett Stained Glass Studios, Inc.   (1898-   )
Philadelphia, Pennsylvania
St. Andrew's Presbyterian Church
5734 West Berwyn Avenue   (5300 North)

Bethlehem Lutheran Church
9401 South Oakley Avenue   (2300 West)

Calvary English Evangelical Church
11249 South Spaulding Avenue   (3300 West)

Chicago Theological Seminary   (Hilton Chapel)
5757 South University Avenue   (1116 East)

Church of the Ascension   (four windows north nave,
   toward altar)
1133 North LaSalle Drive   (150 West)

Church of the Atonement   (chapel window)
5749 North Kenmore Avenue   (1040 West)

Church Home for the Aged
5445 South Ingleside Avenue   (922 East)

Church of Saint Paul and the Redeemer
   (south transept and narthex windows)
4949 South Dorchester Avenue   (1400 East)

East Side Methodist Church
11000 South Ewing Avenue   (3634 East)

Edison Park Evangelical and Reformed Church
6626 North Oliphant Avenue   (7800 West)

Faith Evangelical Lutheran Church
8300 South Sangamon Street   (932 West)

First Baptist Church
4220 West 18th Street

First Presbyterian Church
   (three windows above altar)
6400 South Kimbark Avenue   (1300 East)

Grace Episcopal Church
33 West Jackson Boulevard   (300 South)

Immanuel Lutheran Church
2145 North Maplewood Avenue   (2524 West)

St. James Episcopal Cathedral   (several nave windows)
65 East Huron Street   (700 North)

St. Mary of Nazareth Hospital
   (window in small chapel)
2333 West Division Street   (1200 North)

Morgan Park Presbyterian Church
11056 South Longwood Drive   (1826 West)

North Park College
5125 North Spaulding Avenue   (3300 West)

St. Paul's Union Church
1960 West 94th Street

St. Thomas Lutheran Church
8001 South Jeffery Avenue   (2000 East)

Wright, R. Toland Cleveland, Ohio

First Presbyterian Church (nave windows)
6400 South Kimbark Avenue (1300 East)

Greater Mt. Vernon Baptist Church
  (formerly Our Redeemer Lutheran Church)
6430 South Harvard Avenue (319 West)

Zettler, F. X., Royal Bavarian Art Institute
Munich, Germany

St. Adalbert Church
1656 West 17th Street

All Saints—St. Anthony Church
2849 South Wallace Street (600 West)

The Assumption Greek Orthodox Church
601 South Central Avenue (5600 West)

St. Benedict Church
2201 West Irving Park Road (4000 North)

St. Clara—St. Cyril Church
6401 South Woodlawn Avenue (1200 East)

Corpus Christi Church
4900 South Martin Luther King Drive (400 East)

St. Edmund Church
188 South Oak Park Avenue
Oak Park, Illinois

St. Hyacinth Church
3635 West George Street (2900 North)

Hyde Park Union Church (one nave window)
5600 South Woodlawn Avenue (1200 East)

St. John the Baptist Church
905 West 50th Place

St. Josaphat Church (nave windows)
2301 North Southport Avenue (1400 West)

St. Joseph Church
1731 West 48th Street

St. Mary of the Lake Church
4200 North Sheridan Road (1000 West)

St. Mel—Holy Ghost Church
4301 West Washington Boulevard (100 North)

St. Michael Roman Catholic Church
8237 South Shore Drive (3132 East)

St. Paul Church
2234 South Hoyne Avenue (2100 West)

St. Stanislaus Kostka Church
1327 North Noble Street (1400 West)

St. Thomas Aquinas Church
5112 West Washington Boulevard (100 North)

Glossary

annealing   the last cooling and hardening process in the manufacture of stained glass.

antique glass   glass made today in imitation of medieval glass.

baptistry   part of a church, or as separate building, used for baptisms.

blowpipe   a long hollow metal pipe used to gather and blow molten glass.

bonding   fusing glass to glass or oxides to glass by heat.

cabachon   a small convex or concave circle of glass made by machine and sometimes impressed with a pattern.

cames   strips of lead, usually H-shaped, to hold pieces of glass together.

canopy   an elaborate glass frame within a window imitating an architectural niche, usually Gothic.

cartoon   a full-sized drawing of a window enlarged from a sketch. The leadlines are usually indicated on the cartoon.

cathedral glass   machine-rolled sheet glass of a single color, or infused with colors, often textured with hammered, pebbled, rippled, or other grainy effects.

chancel   part of a church used by the clergy and containing an altar and choir.

clerestory   the upper part of a church containing window openings.

crown glass   hand-blown glass spun into a cylinder on a blowpipe, slit lengthwise and twirled into circular shape before it is tapped from the blowpipe.

drapery glass   semi-molten glass pulled, stretched, and twisted until it forms naturalistic drapery folds.

enamel   paint made of powdered glass held together with a bonding agent and fused to glass by heat.

eye window   a circular window without tracery.

epoxy resin   a synthetic adhesive, sometimes white but more often black, used to hold pieces of slab glass together.

favrile glass   a Tiffany patent for glass exposed to metallic fumes and oxides to produce iridescences.

figural-narrative windows   windows containing human figures to relate biblical or secular stories.

firing   heating glass which has been painted to fuse the paint permanently to the glass.

flashed glass   glass with a thin coat of colored glass on one or both sides.

fused glass   pieces of colored glass bonded to clear or white sheet glass to produce a design.

glass   a hard brittle generally transparent material made of the proper proportions of silica, alkali, and another base substance brought to a liquid state by heat and then cooled and annealed.

glass appliqué   small pieces of glass bonded with white epoxy to sheet glass to form a design.

glass jewels   small pieces of colored glass mechanically faceted or irregularly chipped.

grisaille   from the French "to paint or to make gray." Delicate floral or geometric patterns painted in dark oxides over transparent or translucent glass to subdue light.

lancet   a tall narrow window with a pointed arch.

light   a window opening between mullions, (see mullion).

lunette   a semicircular space over a door or window, or a window to fit such a space.

medallion window   a window designed in small diamonds, circles, squares, or other geometric shapes which contains biblical figures usually arranged in a story-telling sequence.

muff glass   hand-blown like crown glass but when slit and tapped from the blowpipe is square rather than round.

mullion   a vertical shaft of stone which separates window lights.

nave   the main part of a church extending from the entrance to the transept or choir.

occhio window   an eye window which carries a single scene or idea.

opalescent glass glass containing whorls or striations of color. When annealed it has a milky iridescent appearance like that of opals.

oxide a mixture of iron oxide and/or powdered glass which when diluted is used to paint glass.

plating a system of leading one piece of glass behind another to achieve richness and density of color not found in a single sheet of glass.

pot metal glass antique glass of a single color.

pressed glass small bits of glass pressed mechanically into a mold to produce patterned or unpatterned cabachons (see cabachon).

rose window a circular window with design and tracery radiating outward like flower petals from a corolla.

roundel a circular or semicircular piece of glass.

silver stain another name for silver nitrate which when fused to clear glass imparts various shades of yellow.

slab glass glass usually one inch thick, often chipped or faceted and set into epoxy resin or concrete.

strapwork interlacing bands forming geometric patterns in glass.

tracery ornamental work of wood or stone in the upper part of a Gothic window.

transept projecting arms found between the nave and chancel to effect the cruciform plan of a church.

transparent glass glass which permits the transmission of light and allows a clear view of objects behind it.

translucent glass glass which permits the transmission of light but does not allow a clear view of objects behind it.

wash a thin coat of paint to subdue light as well as to delineate objects.

Index

Index *continued*

Photo Credits

Erne R. Frueh: 17, 21, 23, 28, 39, 51 (top and bottom), 59, 61 (top), 65, 67, 75, 76, 79, 80, 81, 98, 100, 101, 102, 103, 105 (top), 107, 109, 111, 117, 119, 122, 123, 125, 130, 139 (top and bottom).

George A. Lane: 5, 8, 11, 15, 35, 37, 45, 47, 49, 54, 55, 56, 57, 61 (bottom), 63, 68, 69, 71, 73, 77, 85, 86, 87, 91, 93, 95, 105 (bottom), 113, 114, 115, 118, 121, 126, 127, 129, 131, 133, 134, 135, 137, 141, 143.

Art Institute of Chicago: 82, 83.

About this book

Chicago Stained Glass was designed by Mary Golon. It was set by Lakeshore Typographers, Inc. The text is 11 on 13 Garamond Book Roman; the captions are 9 on 10 Garamond italic. The book was printed by R. R. Donnelley and Sons Company on Warren's 100-pound Lustro Offset Enamel paper.